WINNING SWEEPSTAKES

The Proven Strategy

Jeffrey & Robin Sklar

To our daughter, Stephanie

Published by
Sebell Publishing Company, Inc.
965 Concord Street
Framingham, MA 01701

Revised Edition 1990

ISBN 0-944159-001 (previously published by Perigee Books, a division of the Putnam Publishing Group)

Printed in the United States of America

2 3 4 5 6 7 8 9 10

Contents

Introduction

We chose *Winning Sweepstakes: The Proven Strategy*, as the title of this book because there is no one magic "system" or secret that in itself guarantees that you will win every time you enter a sweepstakes. There is however, an approach, a strategy, that leads to winning more sweepstakes prizes more often. We call this the *"Winning Sweepstakes Strategy."*

In chapters 1 through 9, we'll tell you the tips, tricks and techniques that taken together, are proven methods for winning sweepstakes. We'll explain how each and every sweepstakes is different and which sweepstakes offer superior odds of winning, how to enter them and how to win them. We'll present a strategy that you can use to win time and again.

In the world of sweepstakes, there is *almost* no such thing as a sure-thing. We say "almost" because our "four-star rated" sweepstakes are the closest thing. Certain fixed odds, game sweepstakes are by far the most lucrative of all sweepstakes. We have never lost a four-star sweepstakes. We'll show you everything you need to know to recognize and win them.

In chapter 10, we'll tell you how to win skill contests. And in chapter 12, we'll give you the straight scoop on how to win at state lotteries - something you won't find in any book that's been written on the subject.

Enjoy the journey ahead. Winning sweepstakes is euphoric, great fun and lucrative.

1. The Sweepstakes Game

Success is a journey, not a destination. - Ben Sweetland

This year over one billion (that's, $1,000,000,000.00) will be awarded in sweepstakes prizes. Hundreds of millions of dollars more will be won in state lotteries and contests. Individual sweepstakes are often worth several million dollars each. Sears, for example, offered $13 million in prizes; Publishers Clearing House and American Family Publishers offer not ungenerous multimillion dollar prizes. With over 3,000 annual sweepstakes in the United States more people are playing sweepstakes than ever before.

What this means is that sweepstakes are more popular - and more profitable - than ever. A lot of people are winning a lot of money. Have you been a winner recently? If not, perhaps you haven't been introduced to the strategies and techniques that can improve your sweepstakes odds.

Winning sweepstakes is not difficult - if you know the winning strategies. The strategies we have evolved over the years have helped us to win tens of thousands of dollars in prizes. With our Winning Sweepstakes Newsletter, we've been able to pass along our winning strategies to thousands of other sweepstakes players. Their success rate has been phenomenal. In a recent subscriber survey we learned that over 50 percent of Winning Sweepstakes Newsletter subscribers had won at least one major sweepstakes prize in the past twelve months. Of those subscribers that submitted at least 10 entries per month, over 90% had won a major sweepstakes prize in the past year. This extraordinary success was accomplished by subscribers entering the sweepstakes that had superior odds of winning. Winning Sweepstakes Newsletter rates sweepstakes for their "winnability".

Winning Sweepstakes: The Proven Strategy offers for the first time in book form our years of research and analysis, presented in a sweepstakes program that can help make you a winner.

If you are now (or were at one time) skeptical about your ability to win sweepstakes, you're not alone.

Prior to April 17, 1980, we had never entered a sweepstakes. We had never mailed in a Publisher's Clearing House or American Family Publisher's or Reader's Digest sweepstakes entry. We had never mailed in a 3" x 5" entry or played the sweepstakes scratch-off type games at McDonald's. We were so skeptical of the long odds and credibility of sweepstakes, that we would throw away the game piece inside the box of breakfast cereal without ever playing it.

Couple the long odds and our dubious opinion of the credibility of sweepstakes with the time and cost of entering, and the result was two confirmed sweepstakes skeptics. "What happened?" you may rightly ask. How did two people who had never entered sweepstakes become sweepstakes converts, regular sweepstakes players and frequent sweepstakes winners?

How We Got Started In Sweepstakes

Jeff's interest in sweepstakes began on April 17, 1980. He was a frequent reader of the Wall Street Journal. In the Business Bulletin column on page 1 of the Journal there was a short blurb about airline game sweepstakes being run at the time by United, TWA and American Airlines. One sentence in that blurb forever changed his perception of sweepstakes.

The sentence read, "...As sales promotion contests can't require a purchase as a condition of entry, the carriers must mail a free chance to anyone who asks."

In other words, you do not have to buy the sponsors product to enter. "That's incredible," Jeff thought, "To get a game card, all you have to do is ask."

Up until that time it had been Jeff's impression that you had to buy the box of Cheerios to get the game card inside. Companies just don't give away prizes to anyone ... or so he thought! What possible benefit could there be for United to give away something for nothing? Without a thorough understanding of sweepstakes and how they work, Jeff was intrigued by the Journal claim and carefully examined its implications ...

- Companies give away free prizes in sweepstakes.
- You can usually get an entry by buying the sponsor's product.
- But ... you don't have to buy anything to enter.
- If you ask, you are entitled to a free entry!

Now here's the key ... each sweepstakes entry has some inherent value. That is, some of the entries win valuable prizes. If $100 in prizes was being given away and there were 100 entries, each entry would have an expected value of $1. If each entry was worth $1 and costs you nothing, you would want as many entries as possible. You could win up to $100 and you couldn't lose!

Of course, life isn't so simple. Although you don't have to pay anything to the sponsor to enter, this does not mean that you do not have to pay to enter. In fact, there are costs. To mail an entry, you need an envelope and postage. Entries also take time and effort. In fact, some entries take double postage, double envelopes, double time and double effort. To get a game piece by mail for instance, you must send in a self-addressed stamped envelope.

Since envelopes can be purchased for a penny or less and the cost of free time and effort is discretionary, Jeff focused on the predominant monetary cost, first class postage. On the basis of postage costs alone, He wondered if any sweepstakes were worth entering as an investment.

Investment Vs. Gamble

In our society, things that involve risk are described as either investments or gambles. Below are the definitions of investment and gamble from Webster's New World Dictionary.

Investment: To put money into business, real estate, stocks, bonds, etc. for the purpose of earning an income or profit. To spend (time, effort, etc.) with the expectation of some satisfaction.

Gamble: To play games of chance for money or some other stake. To take a risk in order to gain some advantage. An act or undertaking involving a risk of loss.

Investments have an upbeat, upscale and prosperous image. Gambles have a downscale, impoverished, down and out reputation. Investors are prudent. Gamblers are reckless. (Texas Savings and Loan bankers guised as investors were actually gamblers, but that's another book).

To the extent that sweepstakes are games of chance, they are gambles. However, as we will explain in this book, some sweepstakes entries are indeed reckless gambles and others are prudent (and very lucrative) investments.

For the purposes of our discussion in this book, we define "investments" as any prize competition in which the average prize value of each entry is *greater* than the cost of each entry.

"Gambles" are prize competitions in which the average prize value of each entry is *less* than the cost of each entry.

To understand the difference between investments and gambles, think of sweepstakes in the following way. If every entry that was submitted into a sweepstakes was yours, which would be greater, the total value of all your prize wins or your total postage cost of submitting all your entries? Anytime you have the long run expectation of winning more than your entry cost, we call this a sweepstakes investment. Anytime you have the long run expectation of winning less than your entry cost, we call this a sweepstakes gamble.

In the long run, sweepstakes investments have an expected positive return on your postage risked, sweepstakes gambles have an expected negative return on your postage risked.

Our First Sweepstakes Investment: TWA Win The World

Shortly after reading the blurb in the Wall Street Journal, the TWA "WIN THE WORLD" SWEEPSTAKES was advertised in the Boston Globe. TWA was giving away 10,000 free round trip flights anywhere in the world with two stop overs. Winners could build their own fantasy trip and visit London, Paris and Rome! The total retail value of each prize was $2000. Below the advertising copy headlines, the official rules were printed in small type. In the small type, was the following line: *The odds of winning are 1 in 300.* 1 in 300 is phenomenal odds.

To obtain an entry (a TWA "Win The World" game card), you had to send a self-addressed stamped envelope to the sweepstakes agency handling the promotion for TWA. At the time, first class postage was 15 cents. So, one entry costs 30 cents for round trip postage.

From the information printed in the rules, Jeff calculated the following:

cost of obtaining one game card	$0.30
total prize value of all cards	$20,000,000
# of game cards printed	3,000,000
average prize value of each game card	$6.67
chance of winning once with 1 game card:	0.33%
chance of winning at least once with 100 game cards:	28%
chance of winning at least once with 200 game cards:	49%
chance of winning at least once with 300 game cards:	67%
chance of winning at least twice with 300 game cards:	28%

These numbers were startling. In this sweeps, every 30 cents invested would, on average, provide us with one game card worth $6.67. Considering postage costs alone, our expected return on investment from this sweeps would be an outrageous 2123%!

We must say that although Jeff found what appeared to be an incredible opportunity, neither of us had any intention of going through the effort to submit entries. Indeed, finding a sweepstakes with such wonderful odds seemed to be a good story in itself.

On April 20th, Jeff created some tables and plotted graphs representing our probabilities of winning (see TWA Graph). The next day Jeff showed the calculations to some friends.

Every person he showed the calculations to had the same response. The first reaction was "you made a mistake, the odds can't be that good." So he reviewed the calculations and indeed our friends agreed -- the figures were correct.

The next objection was "the judging organization made a mistake. There must have been a misprint, the odds of winning cannot be that good." So he called the sweepstakes judging organization in New York and confirmed the printed odds.

Finally, he was told that sweepstakes are fixed. The skeptics said, "If you don't fly the airline, you can't win. Even if they do send you the game cards by mail -- they'll just send you the

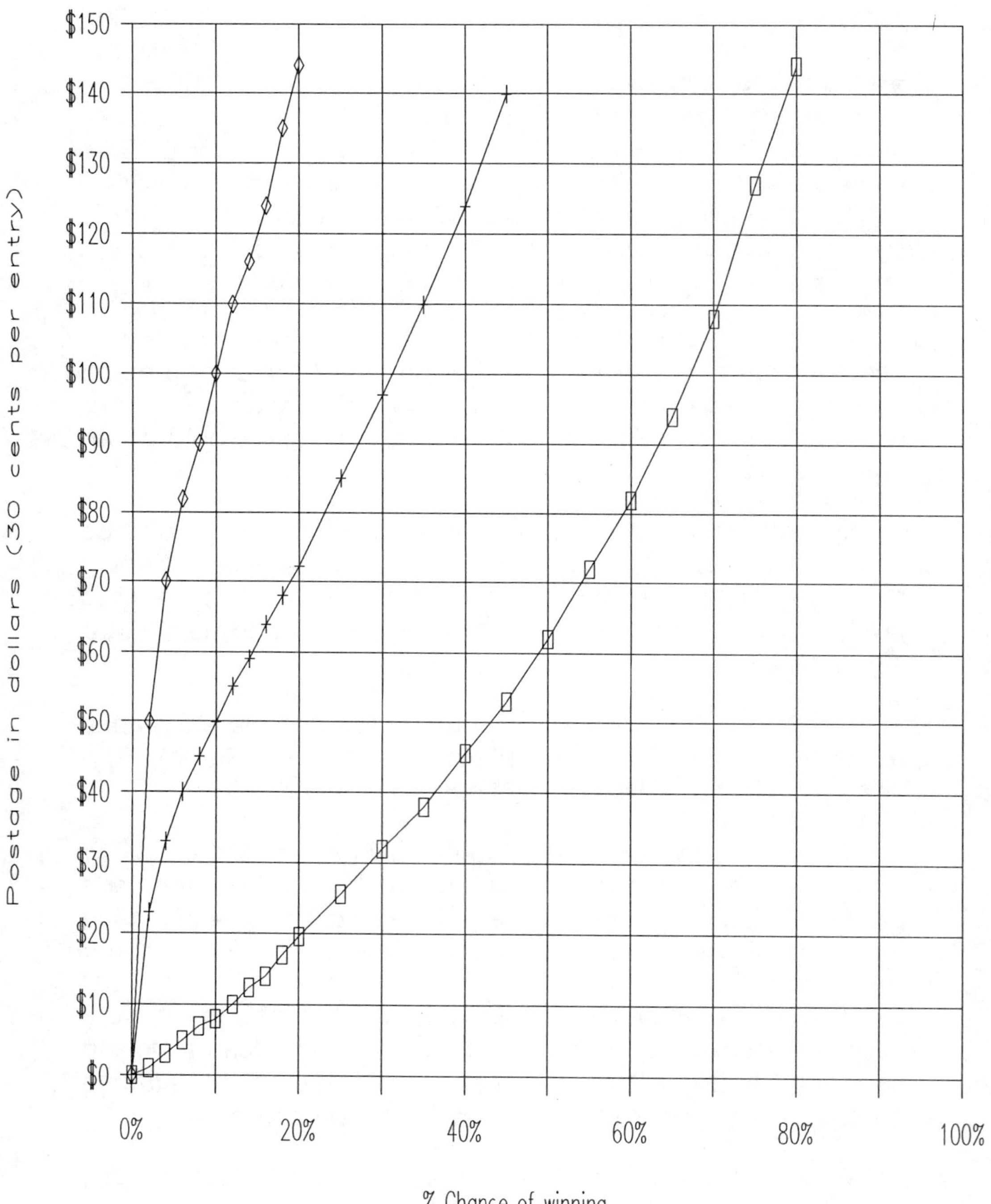
TWA WIN THE WORLD SWEEPSTAKES
Postage in dollars (30 cents per entry)
$150
$140
$130
$120
$110
$100
$90
$80
$70
$60
$50
$40
$30
$20
$10
$0
0%
20%
40%
60%
80%
100%
% Chance of winning
◆ = 1 or more wins
+ = 2 or more wins
□ = 3 or more wins

losing cards. The winning cards will be saved for those who actually fly the planes."

We were unsure of the integrity of sweepstakes but had a sense that they must be somehow regulated -- and honest. After all we reasoned, it they weren't, sweepstakes be out of business when the dishonesty was publicly revealed.

At that point we were challenged to enter the TWA sweepstakes and win. With pride on the line we entered. And won a round trip flight anywhere TWA flies with two stop overs. Not bad for our first effort.

We should add, however, that we came within a whisker of not winning anything at all. We had sent 300 requests for game cards to the sweepstakes judging company. The cards trickled back through the mail. We agreed to accumulate the game cards and scratch them when we were both together. When the first 100 cards were in, we scratched them with Jeff's family, the Sklar's. No winners.

When the second 100 cards came in, we scratched them with Robin's family, the Sebell's. Again, no winners. Our sweepstakes endeavor was becoming a running joke with our families. Almost everyday, Jeff's brother, Frank, would kiddingly tell people that we had won just to get a reaction.

Towards the end, there was a sense of desperation. Game card scratching wasn't much fun. Rather than waiting for a family game card scratching get together, we sometimes scratched the cards when the mail man delivered them. On the 273rd card, Jeff scratched a winner and nearly went berserk. Not wanting to take the thrill away from Robin, He carefully reinserted the winner into another envelope and sealed it shut. That evening we scratched the last cards with the Sebell's.

Since Jeff was guilty of the "unauthorized" scratching of cards that afternoon, he was relegated to passing them out. When the 299th card was scratched without a winner, everyone (except

Jeff, of course) was disappointed. Robin insisted that she be permitted to scratch the last card.

We'll never forget the jubilation that followed. We suspect it was a lot like winning the seventh game of a World Series. We left it to Frank to tell the Sklar's -- nobody believed him. Jeff's grandfather claims that, "Winners always sleep well" but we were all too excited to sleep well that night.

We began to wonder if there were more sweepstakes like the TWA game.

23 Flights Around The World

Over the next few years, we compiled in an impressive string of wins culminating with the $7,000,000 Air Florida Birthday Giveaway promotion. After our TWA winnings, our friends asked that we let them know when the next super sweepstakes came along.

On October 4, 1982, while falling asleep watching the Independent Network News, Jeff thought he heard a commercial for an Air Florida Birthday Sweepstakes that sounded similar to the TWA Promotion. When he awoke the next morning Jeff wasn't sure if he had dreamt about the sweepstakes or if it was real.

Before breakfast he called Air Florida's toll free number. Not surprisingly, the representative was more interested in selling Jeff a ticket on Air Florida than giving him details about the $7,000,000 Birthday Giveaway. Jeff did get enough information to learn that the sweepstakes was real and made a trip to Boston's Logan International Airport to see a copy of the rules.

Later that day, he was standing in front of the Air Florida ticket counter reading the sweepstakes display for the Air Florida Birthday Giveaway. It was between flights and the terminal was nearly empty. As he read the rules, a chill passed through Jeff. He knew what we were about to win. We made photocopies of the rules and distributed them to all of our friends and family. We told everybody we knew about the sweepstakes and recommended that everyone enter.

For that sweepstakes, entrants were allowed to submit only one entry per day from any one address. It was an interesting sweepstakes in many regards. The sweepstakes went on for only six weeks and Air Florida was giving away a total of 12,000 free flights. It was a game sweepstakes, and by checking the rules we discovered that 267,000 game cards had been printed. This meant that the average value of each game card was $26.21 (almost 4 times as valuable as the TWA game cards). As the cost of obtaining a game card at the time was forty cents for postage (the cost of requesting a game piece by mail and a self-addressed, stamped envelope for its return), this was another phenomenal sweepstakes. The expected return on postage risked was 6552%.

cost of obtaining 1 game card	$0.40
# of top prizes	12,000
total prize value of all cards	$7,000,000
# of game cards printed	267,000
average value of a game card	$26.21
chance of winning once with 1 game card:	4.4%

Using simple math, we calculated that our chance of winning one prize with a single game piece was 4.4 percent. With 600 entries (at a total cost of $240 for postage) we calculated our odds of winning as follows:

odds of winning at least 16 prizes	99.2%
odds of winning at least 20 prizes	93.5%
odds of winning at least 24 prizes	74.8%
odds of winning at least 28 prizes	44.6%
odds of winning at least 32 prizes	18.4%
Expected number of flights to win:	26.6

We calculated that one in every 22.25 game cards would win a free air travel prize. We knew that we had a 99% percent chance of winning at least sixteen prizes (flights), and that most likely we would win twenty-six or twenty-seven flights.

On October 5th, we mailed out our first batch of game card requests and had made a full round of calls to all the friends who had asked for the next super sweepstakes tip. Despite our advance recommendations, our friends (and family members) still did not believe that the sweepstakes was winnable. None of them entered!

We wound up winning twenty-three tickets, 110 days of auto rentals, 110 one-day cruises, and over 300 in-flight cocktails. Less than expected but still not a bad return on our investment! Few people commiserated with the fact that we actually won *less* than expected! On one of our free flights we gave away drinks "on the plane" to our fellow passengers. One stewardess told us that it was the most enjoyable flight she'd ever flown.

We have found that there are many "winning sweepstakes." By "winning sweepstakes," we mean a sweepstakes with excellent prizes and a good chance of winning them. On the other hand, there are many losing sweepstakes -- sweepstakes not worth the postage investment. There is no magical "system" that will guarantee a win with every entry but there are concrete strategies that you can use to dramatically improve your chances of winning.

Since our initial success, we've gone on to win tens of thousands of dollars in prizes. We've been featured on Nightline, The Today Show, NBC News, PM Magazine, and The Wall Street Journal Report, and have been written up or interviewed in dozens of newspapers and magazines, from the Boston Globe to Money Magazine.

We were literally swamped with requests for information about the best sweepstakes to enter. Right around the time of the Air Florida wins we began publishing WINNING

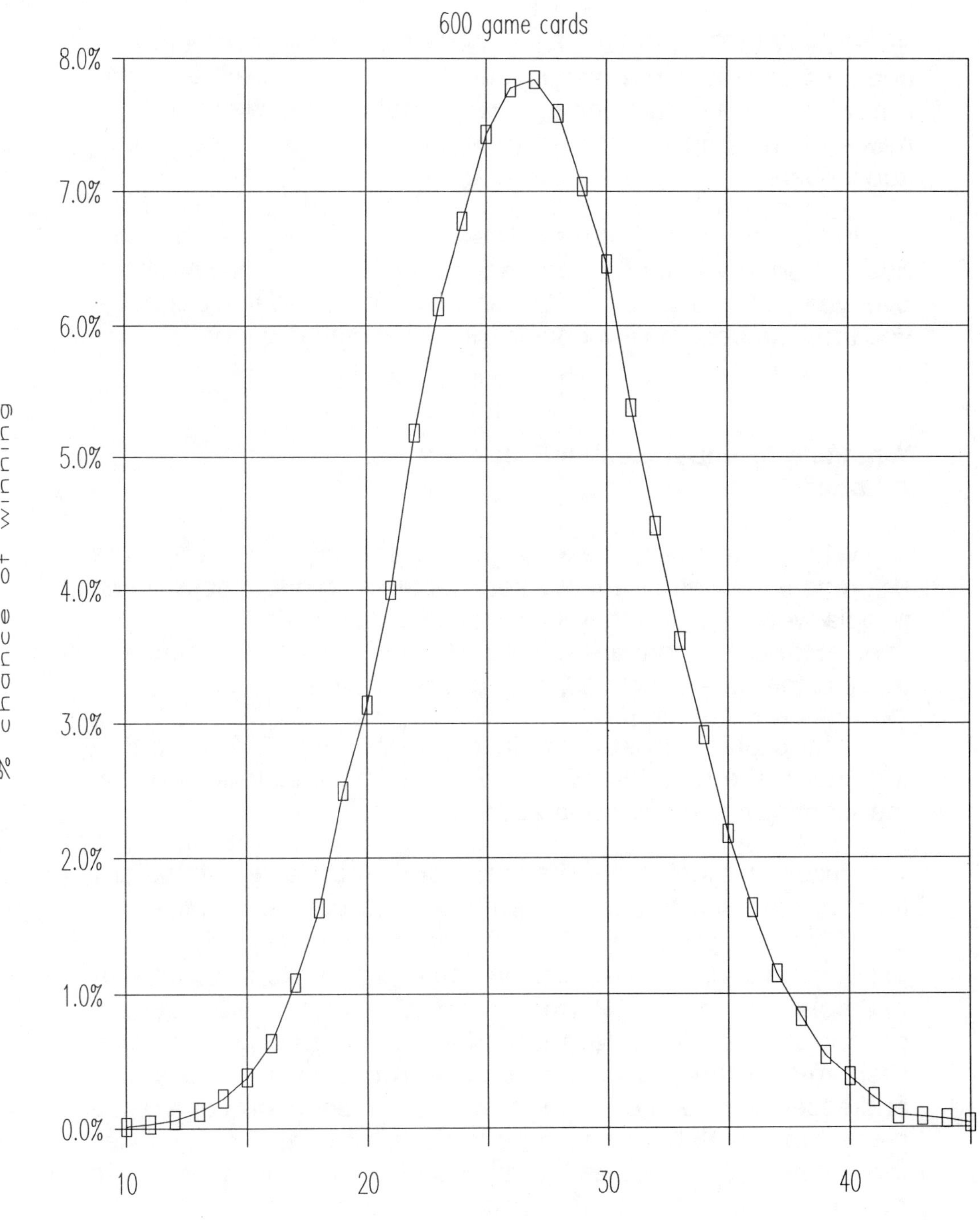

Air Florida Game
600 game cards
8.0%
7.0%
6.0%
5.0%
4.0%
3.0%
2.0%
1.0%
0.0%
% chance of winning
10
20
30
40
# of free tickets

SWEEPSTAKES NEWSLETTER. WSN is the only newsletter that analyzes and rates the sweeps and tells you which are the best to enter. Each month Winning Sweepstakes Newsletter brings news of the important and profitable sweepstakes to our subscribers.

In *Winning Sweepstakes: The Proven Strategy*, we are now passing on to you the tips and advice that we have accumulated over years of sweepstakes play. By following these tips diligently, you too, can become a winner in the sweepstakes game.

What Is a Sweepstakes? A Contest? A Lottery?

What is a sweepstakes? you might ask. What are the differences between sweepstakes, contests, and lotteries? Most people would tell you that they are different names for the same thing. However, there are specific differences between them, and these differences affect your chances of winning.

United States postal regulations state three elements that together make up a lottery: a prize, a factor of luck determining the winner(s), and a consideration.

Prizes and luck are self-explanatory. A consideration is any form of payment required to enter a prize competition that is a benefit to the sponsor (such as the price of a lottery ticket). The exact definition of consideration varies from state to state. For example, the laws of Vermont and Washington state regard postage as a "consideration" (i.e., a payment); therefore, residents of these states cannot be required to send a self-addressed, stamped envelope to receive an entry form or a game piece. In most states, postage is not a consideration because the sponsor does not derive revenue from it. It is important to note that in the United States, lotteries can be run only by the government or by sanctioned charities (lotteries run by charities are known as raffles).

Contests differ from lotteries in that they eliminate the element of luck. They do offer prizes, of course. And they may or may not require a consideration (often a contestant has to purchase the sponsor's product to enter). The element of luck is eliminated because contests require some skill, such as the ability to compose a jingle in twenty-five words or less. In this case, the best or most skillful jingle wins.

Sweepstakes feature prizes and luck - but unlike lotteries, sweepstakes do *not* require a consideration. No purchase is necessary to enter or win a sweepstakes. The sweepstakes format provides the chance to get something for *nothing*, and this is the primary reason that sweepstakes have become so popular.

Is There a Gimmick to Winning Sweepstakes?

Jeff Sklar: "The first comment on sweepstakes made by Ted Koppel when Jeff was interviewed on Nightline was, 'You had to wonder about the gimmick. I mean nobody gives away $50,000 or $100,000 ... or $2 million without a gimmick.'"

What is the "gimmick"? The gimmick behind sweepstakes is that sponsors know that when a sweepstakes is run, the lure of something for nothing will cause consumers to examine the sponsor's products more closely. The sponsor hopes to attract new customers. This is the silent "understanding" between consumers and sponsors. In exchange for considering the sponsor's product, the consumer is given the opportunity to win a prize.

An advertiser uses a sweepstakes to draw attention to his product so that the product may sell itself. And in today's American society, any advertising tool that commands attention is desperately needed by advertisers. In the book, *Positioning:*

The Battle For Your Mind by Al Ries and Jack Trout, the authors point out that:

- The average supermarket stocks over 12,000 food products or brands.
- The 1500 companies listed on the New York stock exchange introduce over 5000 new products annually.
- Each year 30,000 new books are published in the United States.
- There are over a half million active trademarks at the U.S. Patent Office. And there are over 25,000 new trademarks filed every year.

And sweepstakes have proven to be an effective means of making a product (or service) stand apart from the crowd. Some of the marketing motivations for running sweepstakes are:

- Advertising Power. The average American is exposed to thousands of paid advertisements every day, ranging from the logos on the jerseys of professional tennis players to television commercials. Sweepstakes are another kind of advertising. In a Johnnie Walker sweepstakes, entrants had to phone a toll-free number and listen to a thirty-second message about the virtues of Johnnie Walker. American Greetings used a sweepstakes that required entrants to watch its television commercial in order to learn the sweepstakes "qualifier" (a qualifier is a proof of purchase or a word or phrase that is hand-printed on a piece of paper; when required, a qualifier must accompany each sweepstakes entry).

  The cable network Lifetime sponsored the "$400,000 Chance of a Lifetime Sweepstakes" to attract new viewers. Lifetime distributed millions of match-type game pieces through program guides and local cable mailings. The matching symbols were shown only during Lifetime programs. If you wanted to win their sweeps, it was necessary to watch their programs.

- Positive Association. Sweepstakes establish goodwill with consumers. Sponsors like you to think of winning when you think of their product.

- Excitement. Marketers know that a chance to win $25,000 in a sweepstakes is more exciting to consumers than a twenty-five cent coupon.

- Better Display Space. Sweepstakes frequently help manufacturers to get better display space for their products in stores. Better display space in turn, sells more product.

- Target Marketing. By offering certain types of prizes, sponsors can aim their sweepstakes at a specific audience. A pharmaceutical company once ran a sweepstakes offering insulin products as prizes. Since only diabetics were likely to enter the promotion, the sweepstakes yielded a valuable list of potential customers.

- Educate Consumers about a Product. If a baby-oil company wants its audience to know that its product is good for sun tanning, it might run a sweeps offering trips to warm climates complete with a large supply of complimentary baby oil.

- Introduction of a New Product or Process. When Wells Fargo and Shawmut Banks of Boston wanted to make their customers more familiar with their ATM's (automatic teller machines), the banks ran sweepstakes in which ATM transactions automatically entered customers in the banks' sweepstakes.

- To Test Consumer Response. Sweepstakes and contests sponsored by MTV consistently draw huge numbers of entrants. The phenomenal response to these promotions has shown advertisers that MTV viewers are responsive viewers. This has helped MTV sell advertising time.

- To Present a Positive Image. Sweepstakes provide a way for companies to build a positive image for themselves. McDonald's used game sweepstakes to promote its association with the Olympics. Every time the United States won a medal, game players won free food and other prizes.

- Increase Coupon Redemption. Studies have shown that coupons that double as automatic sweepstakes entries have a higher redemption rate than coupons without sweepstakes offers.

- Direct Mail Response. If a sweepstakes is included in a mail package, people look more closely at the materials inside. Direct marketers have successfully through testing that sweepstakes boost mailing response rates.

Kraft sponsored a video game sweepstakes that reportedly boosted sales of Kraft's Handi-Snacks by at least 40% during the February - March 1990 sales period. After Marine Midland bank learned from its ad agency that 70% of all Americans play lotteries or enter sweepstakes, they sponsored a sweepstakes that led to a reported 22% increase in bank loans.

You should understand that it is possible for a sweepstakes sponsor to give you something for no cost but still get something in return. Knowing this, you should not be one of those people who buy a product just to enter a sweepstakes for any of the following reasons:

- Ignorance. Some consumers mistakenly believe that you must buy the sponsor's product to enter.

- Laziness. Sometimes people are too lazy to write away for game pieces. Many players buy a product just to get a game piece instantly.

- Guilt. Some consumers do not feel "entitled" to enter a sweepstakes unless they make a product purchase.

- Suspicion. Some believe that people who enter a sweepstakes without buying anything lose and that buying the sponsor's product helps increase the chance of winning. Sponsors do little to dispel this idea, because it helps them sell. Most sets of fine-print rules detail two methods of entering the sweepstakes, one of which is always free. Sponsors list the method that requires a product purchase first.

Not only are sweepstakes successful marketing tools, but they have also been used for non-marketing purposes. In the past few years, several law enforcement agencies have mailed sweepstakes prize win notification letters to lure suspects into turning themselves in. In March 1990, the Providence, Rhode Island Police Department used this trick to successfully lure 63 persons who failed to make court appearances.

In many ways, sweepstakes also present a way for a sponsor to thank its valued customers. If Coca-Cola could afford to give away a car to every customer, it probably would. Unfortunately, no company can afford to do this so instead they run a sweepstakes and give away only as many cars as they can. The entrant is under no legal obligation to buy anything from the sponsor.

A word of reassurance: in all direct mail sweepstakes offers, the consumer can enter the sweepstakes by responding in one of two ways:

YES! I want to buy your product and enter the sweepstakes.

NO, I do not want to buy your product, but want to enter the sweepstakes anyway.

Mailers sometimes require separate envelopes for "Yes" and "No" responses, knowing that some entrants will think they have a better chance of winning if they buy the product.

Remember: Your chances of winning do not improve if you buy the product - regardless of what the packaging seems to imply. Whether you buy the product or not, your chances of winning remain the same. It is the law.

The Growth of Sweepstakes

In 1976, $63 million in sweepstakes prizes were given away. In every year since, the total value of sweepstakes prizes has steadily increased. This year over one billion in prizes will be awarded.

What are the reasons for the boom in sweepstakes activity?

1. Consumer Acceptance. The smooth operation of state lotteries has lent credibility to sweepstakes prize promotions.

2. Economic Conditions. When the economy slowed down, people looked for opportunities to win big. Sweepstakes and lotteries had a great appeal. When times got better, the sweepstakes hobby was already well established.

3. Changes in the laws. Deregulation and easing of laws in almost every state have permitted continued growth of sweepstakes.

4. Sweepstakes Innovations. Marketers have found new and exciting formats, such as the game sweepstakes, which have dramatically helped meet advertising goals.

Today, there are more prize-winning opportunities than ever before. This is good news for sweepstakes players.

2. Sweepstakes Odds And Ends

"If winning is not important, why keep score?"
- Lt. Commander Worf from Star Trek: The Next Generation

Before we get into the details of the specific types of sweepstakes (and the strategies to win them), you will need to develop a mind set about sweepstakes. In this section, we present a potpourri of sweepstakes winning ideas.

- You must be willing to enter sweepstakes. When describing the willingness of people to take risks, Psychologists classify people into of two categories - those who are risk seekers and those who are risk adverse.

  Risk seekers are people looking for a thrill. They care little for the consequences of their risk taking action.

  Risk adverse people on the other hand, are fearful of risk. Even when it is in their best long term interest to take a risk, risk adverse people will seldom act.

  Smart sweepstakes players should be neither risk seeking nor risk adverse. Instead, they must be what we call, "risk analytical." That is, they weigh the risk and enter (or not enter) accordingly. Smart sweepstakes players do not recklessly submit lots of entries into a sweepstakes without some idea of their likelihood of winning. Smart sweepstakes players also do not refrain from entering the best sweepstakes.

  Successful sweepstakes players are optimists. They know that every entry (except in rare circumstances) will not win. But they know that each entry is an opportunity to win and they anticipate winning every sweepstakes they enter.

- You must play to win. What other possible reason could there be for entering? Some sweepstakes, contests and lottery players claim to play for fun. Whether or not they win is unimportant, they claim. If this is you, just skim through the remainder of this book. If winning is important, you're in the right place. It is our experience that winning and having fun are not mutually exclusive. In fact, winning is great fun!

- You must believe that you can win sweepstakes or you never will. This is not to say that a positive attitude gives entries a better chance of winning. However, if you do not that you can win, you will never have the motivation needed to enter consistently. If you do not enter, you will never win. This we guarantee.

- You must understand that "Someone is going to win, why not me" thinking ... is flawed. While the statement is true, it is also irrelevant. The same statement applies to space stations falling on your house. Although it is possible, it is highly unlikely. It is better to think, "I can improve my chances of winning by picking the right sweepstakes and hope for a little luck rather than being dependent on sheer luck."

  In his best selling book, *Innumeracy*, author John Allen Paulos, discusses the lack of numerical understanding in today's society.

  Paulos cites a Scientific American article referring to the packaging on the Rubik's Cube. On the packaging it states that there are more than 3 billion combinations. In fact, calculations reveal that there are more than 40,000,000,000,000,000,000 combinations. This is equivalent to say that the moon is more than a few feet from the Earth. While the statement is true, it is a massive understatement.

To apply this logic to sweepstakes, it is better to concentrate your entries on winning sweepstakes rather than losing sweepstakes. That is, sweepstakes with better odds are better than sweepstakes with long odds. If a sweepstakes has a negative return on investment, then the sweepstakes is a bad bet ... and not worth entering.

- You must understand that 80%-90% of all national sweepstakes are not worth entering. The key to winning is to be selective and enter only the very best sweepstakes. We'll show you how.

Return on Investment

As discussed in the first chapter, a positive return on investment means that in the long run, you expect to come out ahead. A negative return on investment means that in the long run, you expect to come out behind. Return on investment has nothing to do with your chances of winning. It has only to do with the total prize value and the total number of entries.

Odds

The odds statement 10:1 (against winning) means for every 10 losers, there is 1 winner. This means that you have a 1 in 11 chance of winning.

The Odds and the Return on Investment

The Return on Investment and Odds should be used together as tools to determine whether or not you should enter (and expect to win) a sweepstakes. If the return on investment is positive, consider the odds before you decide to enter. If the return on investment is negative, do not enter (regardless of the odds).

When the return on investment is positive, the odds can help you determine your likelihood of winning in the *short* run.

For example, consider a promotion in which each entry costs you $1 and there is a total of 100 entries for a single prize of $60. The value of each entry is 60 cents ($60 divided by 100 entries). You should not enter because the value of each entry is less than the entry cost ($1). By the way, the odds of winning were 1 in 100 (or 99:1).

If the promotion is changed slightly so that each entry costs you $1, there is a total of 100 entries but instead of a single prize of $60, each entry receives a prize of 60 cents. Would this promotion be worth entering? The value of each entry is less than the entry cost ($1). The answer is no for the same reason. The value of each entry is again, only 60 cents ($60 divided by 100 entries). Even though every single entry wins, the promotion is not worth entering because the return on investment is negative.

Return on investment is more important than the odds. State lotteries frequently advertise the odds of winning but they never advertise the return on investment. If a state lottery were to advertise, "You have a 1 in 5 chance of winning but each $1 ticket is worth only 50 cents," how many people would buy tickets? Only when you have a positive return on investment should you even consider the odds. (NOTE: For the remainder of this book, statements about your odds apply only when the return on investment is positive).

Rule 1: You should never enter a sweepstakes unless you have a positive return on investment.

Rule 2: You should never submit a large number of entries into a sweepstakes unless you have a real possibility of winning with the number of entries you submit.

Long Odds and Luck

The techniques in this book will help you to shorten your odds of winning. Sweepstakes with short odds are easier to win than sweepstakes with long odds. By selecting sweepstakes with short odds to enter, you are making the odds work for you. This will lead to more consistent wins. Winning in general, is however, streaky and sporadic, because you are dependent upon finding high quality sweepstakes to enter.

There is of course, one other sure-fire way to win. That is to have random chance act in your favor (i.e. be lucky). In all things involving chance, a little luck helps. But the less you are dependent upon luck, the more frequently you will win. Selecting the best sweepstakes to enter is a skill.

3. About Sweepstakes

Winning isn't everything, but wanting to win is. - Vince Lombardi

Many years ago there was only one type of sweepstakes - random draw sweepstakes. Entrants submitted their names and addresses on pieces of paper and all the entries were collected in a large drum. At the time of the drawing, the drum was rotated several times to mix the entries, and a blindfolded judge reached into the drum and picked out the names of the winners.

Since that time, sweepstakes have become much more sophisticated. There are now over 150 professional sweepstakes judging companies that create, promote and judge sweepstakes. Random draw sweepstakes themselves have not changed all that much.

The most dramatic change in the sweepstakes world has been the development of new sweepstakes formats. The new formats have a direct effect on the way winners are selected - and on your chances of winning. If you plan to enter sweepstakes regularly, you need to learn the differences between the various kinds of sweepstakes.

Random Draw Sweepstakes

In the traditional random draw sweepstakes, the number of potential entrants is unlimited. Winners are chosen by draw - whether conducted by computer or by picking entries from a drum. Your chances of winning are determined by the number of prizes offered and the number of entries submitted. *Your odds of winning are better when there are more prizes and fewer entries.*

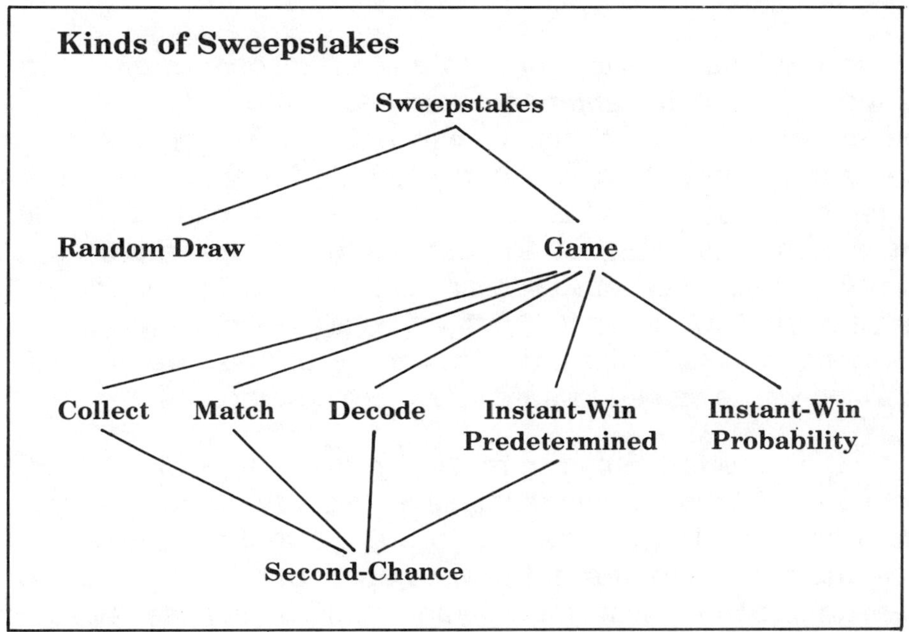

In recent years, there have been some additions to the traditional random draw sweepstakes. Two such variations include multiple draws and radio sweepstakes.

Multiple Draws. Multiple draws are sweepstakes with multiple entry deadlines where winners are chosen after each deadline. Each year for the past few years the Hershey Company has given away $1,000 a day every day in its multiple draw "Scholar Dollar Sweepstakes." Glass Plus gave away $1000 per day for 100 days in the multiple draw Glass Plus "One Hundred Days of Winning!" Sweepstakes.

Every year several major-league baseball teams have sponsored multiple draws in which prizes are awarded every time a home team player hits a home run. Entries are carried over from drawing to drawing, giving an entrant many chances to win. A Baltimore Orioles fan won $1 million in such a sweepstakes in June of 1984.

In multiple draws, if entries are not discarded after each drawing, you should enter early and often. If you do, you will 1) be entered in the early drawings when there are fewer contestants and therefore better odds of winning, and 2) be entered in more drawings and thus have more chances to win. Here is the wording used to describe the multiple drawings for the Glass Plus sweepstakes: "Each entry received before 7/1/90, or between 7/1/90 and 10/8/90, will be eligible for daily drawings still not conducted." It is crucial to know if losing entries from one drawing will be carried forward into future drawings.

Many sports teams run multiple draw sweepstakes offering prizes every time a home team player hits a home run, scores a goal or touchdown. The key to playing these multiple draw sweepstakes is to find out how to enter during the exhibition season or during the first few games. Entries submitted near the deadline for the final drawing have a far smaller chance of winning.

Radio Sweeps. In search of greater listener ship and higher ratings, radio stations give away cash, vacations, cars, concert tickets and other luxuries to keep their faithful listeners and attract new ones. What this means for you, the prize-seeking listener, is great prize winning opportunities.

There are two basic kinds of radio contests: 1) "they call you," and 2) "you call them." In both types, there are specific strategies you can use to enhance your chances of winning.

Usually there are very few restrictions on these giveaways, but occasionally there are restrictions on age or how often you can enter or win.

When the rules are given on the air, pay close attention to them. Many radio stations offer a printed set of rules that is available upon request that apply to all their promotions. You should request a copy from each station you listen to.

"THEY CALL YOU" STRATEGIES

Radio stations frequently run promotions in which they announce a dollar amount or a secret phrase. They randomly call households in the listening area and ask the phone answerer for the amount or phrase. A correct answer leads to financial rewards. We call these "they call you" radio contests.

Usually radio stations select the phone numbers they call randomly from the phone book. In this case, there is little you can do to improve your chances of winning other than knowing the answer the caller will be looking for. However, most stations occasionally pick numbers from mail-in entries. If your number is unlisted or you want to improve your chances of being called, submit mail entries to radio promotions whenever this option is available.

If the radio station calls and you do not know the secret phrase or dollar amount your efforts are wasted. So stick to one radio station promotion at a time so you are guaranteed to be up to date on it. Write down the winning information when it is given and keep this information handy.

If you have a group of friends who are all interested in these giveaways, perhaps each of you could concentrate on one radio station, and share with each other the necessary information. This is one way to stay on top of several giveaways.

Enter the giveaway as soon as it begins. At the beginning of a contest, less promotion has been run and fewer listeners have heard about it. In multiple draw types, early entries will not only have the advantage of being entered in more drawings, but also will be entered in the early drawings where chances of winning are greatest.

Most radio stations run promotions by announcing what prize will be given to a specific number caller. The lucky caller wins the prize. We call these "you call them" giveaways. Here are some tips to increase your chances of winning:

- Concentrate your efforts on suburban radio stations. These tend to have a smaller listening audience and therefore less competition. Also, it is easier to connect to a local call.

  In general, AM talk stations are a better choice than FM rock stations which draw more prize-seeking listeners. Some stations run programs which are not particularly popular. A good hint that a station has a small audience is when they repeat the contest telephone number several times, practically begging for callers. These present much better opportunities for winning.

- Focus on off-peak hours when they are fewer listeners. Good times are early in the morning, late at night and during work and driver commute hours.

- Pay particular attention to the last half of radio programs. Because the stations like to keep their listeners "hanging on" until the end of the program, this is when they more often award prizes.

PHONE AND DIALING STRATEGIES:

- Dial very carefully. You may need to wait several minutes before the telephone is answered. You don't want to be waiting on a wrong number! Many of the newer telephones (even the inexpensive ones) have a redial button. This feature will enable you to dial more quickly and with greater accuracy. If you call the same station frequently you should program the telephone number into your telephone if your phone has this feature. It should go without saying, that rotary dial phones are out and that pushbutton phones are mandatory.

- Assemble a list of phone numbers for the contest lines of all the radio stations you listen to. These phone numbers are seldom changed. Keep a copy by the phone you use for radio contests. Usually the DJ does not give the phone number until he has already announced the contest. You can get a head start on the other listeners if you know the number in advance. Sometimes the numbers are in the phone book, but usually they are not.

- If you can anticipate the contest announcement you can start to dial before the contest is actually announced. Many times a radio giveaway is regularly run at the same time of the day or same day of the week. If you call during the middle of a giveaway program and the line is busy, try to anticipate when an on-air caller will hang up. Remember that most radio stations delay broadcasts by a few seconds.

- If you get a ring or a slow busy signal occasionally, you're in the hunt. And with perseverance, you'll either win sooner (and perhaps often) or later. If you never get anything but a "rapid" busy signal, look for a contest on another radio station. A rapid busy signal means that the phone company's circuits are busy and probably means that there's too much competition.

- If you get through but are not the lucky caller, do not hang up until the line disconnects. On some phone systems, after cycling through all the other phone lines, the DJ will pick up your line again before it disconnects.

REFERENCE MATERIALS

Keep a World Almanac and trivia encyclopedia handy for trivia contests. If there is a sports call-in trivia program in your area, purchase a media guide for each of the major local sports teams. The guides are typically priced around $5 -- they can give you an unbeatable edge. Ask if an older edition is available -- it costs less money and is just as useful.

WHEN YOU WIN

Congratulations! You should be excited. There's nothing quite like the thrill of victory. But more than being ecstatic, SOUND ECSTATIC! Too many radio contest winners sound bored. Radio stations are looking for "sound bites" to replay to promote their contests. And you should give them their booty. After all, you're getting yours!

How Random Drawings Are Conducted

There are so many independent sweepstakes judging organizations that it is not surprising that the process of selecting winners differs from drawing to drawing. Some of the sweepstakes judging organizations consider their process of selecting winners a trade secret.

Sweepstakes judging organizations select the top prize winners first. If bottom prize winners were selected first, it would actually be a disadvantage to be among the first chosen, since those entries would not have a chance at the top prize. With a larger number of entries, they use various random selection techniques. Some of these involve the use of computers and others involve selecting a few entries from each of the many mailbags received. But the actual method used should not affect each entry's chance of winning. Each entry has an equal chance of winning and that is the only vital point to sweepstakes players.

Game Sweepstakes

Game sweepstakes are the fastest growing form of sweepstakes today. The major reason for their popularity is that a sweepstakes player participates in finding out whether or not he or she has won a prize.

Some sweepstakes players view game sweepstakes as the fast food version of "regular" sweepstakes - they remove some of the mystery from sweepstakes. In random draw sweepstakes, one fills out and submits an entry, not certain whether the entry will win or lose. Players are only notified later, if they win. There is no way to know whether you have lost a sweepstakes unless you request a winners list. (We've never heard of a judging organization that notifies the losers.)

In game sweepstakes, the number of prizes and the number of entries are predetermined. The number of entries is determined by the number of game pieces printed. (Only a fixed percentage of the total number of game pieces printed are winners.) The number of people playing a game sweepstakes has no effect on your chances of winning. Either you get a winning card or you do not.

Not all game sweepstakes are the same. There are five types of game sweepstakes: collect, match, decode, and instant-win predetermined and instant-win probability.

Collect. To win the collect game sweepstakes, the entrant must collect game pieces (of which usually one is rare) to spell a word, build a picture, and so forth. Many potential players unwittingly discard the rare piece.

Match. Match game sweepstakes usually involve matching a number or picture from a game piece to a list of winning selections. Typically, the winning selections are posted in retail stores, or can be obtained through the mail.

Decode. Decode game sweepstakes usually instruct the entrant to take his or her game piece to a special decoding display in a store to see if it is a winner. The game pieces are always scrambled so that they can not be read without the "special" decoder. Some new fangled decode sweepstakes require computer equipment to play. In 1989, K Mart put bar codes on store flyers which consumers brought to K Mart stores to be scanned. The computer announced if and what the customer won.

Instant-Win Predetermined. Predetermined instant-win sweepstakes usually feature a game piece from which you scratch off a covering layer, which reveals any prize that may have been won. For example, in scratching a card three panels may be revealed; if all match, the card is a winner. How you scratch the game piece has no affect because the outcome is predetermined.

It is sometimes possible to differentiate winning and losing game pieces prior to playing if the pieces were printed separately. One can look for slight differences such as a filled in letter "e" or a stray dot that might appear only on winning game pieces.

Instant-Win Probability. In probability games, every piece is a potential winner if scratched or played properly. For example, Appian Way Pizza ran a probability instant-win game in which ten spots were covered with a film layer. Two of the ten spots carried matching prizes. If the player could uncover the matching spots with only two scratches, he or she won the prize indicated. Every game card was a potential winner of $5 to $5,000.

In some cases, it is possible to "beat" the game if "patterns" or "keys" can be found in the distribution or design of the game.

"Pattern Strategy": If you can detect a pattern to the location of winning scratch spot locations, this information can be used to increase the probability of winning an instant-win probability game. The application of Pattern Strategy does not make every game piece a winner but does make more pieces winners than would normally be expected by pure chance.

"Key Strategy" is completely breaking a game's code so that you know with certainty where all the winning scratch spot locations are located without scratching them. When applying

"Key Strategy" it is possible to play most (if not all) game pieces into winners.

Depending on the sophistication of the game, it is usually necessary to obtain many game pieces to determine if a pattern or key exists. Prudently designed instant-win probability games have neither patterns nor keys.

Most sponsors are reluctant to run Instant-Win Probability games because the potential prize liability can be astronomical. If 1 million cards are printed and each card could win say, $100, then the potential total prize liability would be $100,000,000 ($100 per card multiplied by 1,000,000 cards). However, worse than this has happened. No responsible executive should allow a company such financial exposure. Further, any executive irresponsible enough to permit his company such exposure, is also probably irresponsible enough to approve the design of a game with patterns or keys.

In 1985, Beatrice Companies sponsored an instant-win probability game, The "Beatrice Monday Night Winning Line-Up" Sweepstakes, in which every game card was a potential winner of $7,000 (in cash). 3,000,000 cards were printed. The potential total prize liability was $21,000,000,000 (that's 21 billion dollars)! If the design and execution of the game were correct, that is, without patterns and keys, then Beatrice would have gotten off the hook and almost assuredly, no one would have won the top prize. In fact, the intended odds were so poor that one could argue that Beatrice's intent was to defraud the public. 70,000 game pieces would had to have been distributed to each person on Earth for there to be a likely chance that the grand prize would have been won. And only 3,000,000 cards were printed.

However, in addition to the incredible potential prize liability, the Beatrice game was flawed with patterns and keys. As a result over $23,000,000 worth of prizes were "won" by players. With a small number of game cards, we "won" eleven nineteen-inch color televisions, four VCR's and one forty-five-inch big screen color TV using Pattern Strategy. Two players, Frank Maggio and

James Curl of Atlanta, used "Key Strategy," hoarded game cards and "won" nearly $20,000,000. At the last minute, Beatrice tried to cancel the game. In the end, all prizes were awarded after a two-year class-action court battle. Frank Maggio and James Curl did not participate in the class-action and settled out of court.

As a matter of practice, we always request a few dozen game cards for all instant-win probability games in search of patterns and keys.

Awarding Prizes in Game Sweepstakes

There are some unique aspects to claiming prizes in game sweepstakes. In collect games, it is necessary to collect several pieces, usually including one that is rare, in order to win. Pepsi Cola ran a collect game using bottle caps as game pieces. Each bottle cap had a letter printed inside. To win this sweepstakes, one had to collect the letters to spell P-E-P-S-I S-P-I-R-I-T. Since not all Pepsi drinkers were collecting the bottle caps, there was a distinct possibility that a consumer could unknowingly discard one of the rare caps. Indeed, this is what happened. In fact, many potential winners unknowingly discard the winning piece in collect game sweepstakes. As a result, prizes frequently go unclaimed.

In general, the more difficult it is to play a game sweepstakes, the more prizes will go unclaimed. In decode and match sweepstakes games, many potential winners do not bother to visit store locations to play their cards.

Instant-win games, on the other hand, are very easy to play. It is not necessary to collect game pieces or use special decoders or visit a store location to find out if you're a winner. Players find out immediately whether they've won or lost. For this reason, people with winning game pieces almost always claim their prizes.

In the early days of game sweepstakes, most of the prizes offered in collect, match, and decode games were not awarded. "Second-chance" sweepstakes were born in 1973 when the Federal Trade Commission challenged the "McDonald's $500,000 Sweepstakes." This "sweeps" was structured in a way that made it very difficult to win. Of the 16,610 possible prizes in the promotion, only 227 were actually awarded - less than 2 percent of the prizes! Outraged FTC staff attorneys challenged McDonald's, arguing that this practice was deceptive.

Today, most sponsors see to it that all prizes are awarded (even when they are not required to do so by law). The most common method for dispensing the unawarded prizes is the "second-chance" sweepstakes. Second-chance sweeps are run like random draw sweepstakes -- regardless of the kind of game sweepstakes run the first time around. It is not uncommon in decode, match, and collect games for the majority of prizes to be left unclaimed and awarded in the second chance.

Because second-chance sweepstakes tend to attract very few entrants, they are among the most lucrative sweepstakes opportunities available.

How to Obtain Game Pieces in Game Sweepstakes

There are two ways to obtain sweepstakes game pieces. The easiest (and usually the most expensive) way to obtain pieces is to purchase a product with a game piece enclosed. Game pieces are typically distributed at a point of sale, in a newspaper insert or packed with a product (inside the box or under a lid, for example).

The alternative method is to send away for them, and this option is almost always available. The standard procedure to request game pieces is simply to send a self-addressed, stamped envelope to the address listed in the rules. The sponsor will recognize your request because you will be mailing to a special address set up for such requests. The cost of obtaining a sweepstakes game piece, therefore, is the price of two first-class stamps (for round trip postage to and from the sponsor). Occasionally sending away for game pieces is not the least expensive way of obtaining them. In sweepstakes sponsored by candy bar makers, for example, the cost of the candy bar is often less than the cost of postage.

It is a good idea to print the name of the sweepstakes and the date mailed on your *stamped, self-addressed* reply envelope. This way, you'll know how long it took for the requested materials to be fulfilled. Also, if the sweepstakes game materials are not self-explanatory, you'll know what sweepstakes they came from.

Sweepstakes Myths

Mythstake 1. *"I don't believe in sweepstakes -- there's always a catch. Prizes are never awarded."*

Not true. Prizes are awarded and virtually all sweeps are on the level. If they weren't, leading companies would not have anything to do with them. Why would a company needlessly risk its reputation on a giveaway? When prizes are not given away, it's often because winning game pieces were not sent in by the public. Even then, there are often second-chance reruns to try to give away all prizes.

Mythstake 2. *"All sweepstakes require an official entry blank. Sometimes I can't find one."*

Over 90 percent of all sweepstakes do not require an official entry blank to enter or win. You can usually enter by printing the necessary information on a plain piece of paper or a card. When an official entry form is required, often it is available by mail.

Mythstake 3. *"I have to buy something to win."*

Absolutely untrue. You do not need to make a purchase in order to enter - or win - a sweepstakes. The odds of winning are the same whether a purchase is made or not. If buying a product improved your chances of winning, the purchase would be regarded as a consideration, which would make the sweepstakes an illegal lottery.

Mythstake 4. *"You never know if you've won. You have to write for a winners list."*

Not true. Sweepstakes judging organizations must tell you if you've won. Most judging organizations make great efforts to reach you. After all, winners are good publicity for sponsors.

Mythstake 5. *"If the game is going on in another state, I can't enter."*

Some sweeps are regional or exclude some geographical areas, but most are open to anyone in the United States.

Mythstake 6. *"Sweepstakes only allow one entry per person."*

There are sweepstakes that permit only one entry per person or per family. Some permit one entry per day. But many permit multiple entries. The more entries you submit, the better your chances of winning. This book will help you evaluate the sweepstakes worth sending multiple entries to.

Mythstake 7. *"One sweepstakes is the same as another - it doesn't matter which I enter."*

This is the biggest "myth" of all! All sweepstakes are not created equal. Some sweepstakes offer more great prizes - to a smaller number of people - over a shorter period of time and thus offer a better chance of winning. One of the key lessons of this book is how to choose the best sweepstakes to enter.

Most people think the odds of winning any sweepstakes are extremely long. Sometimes this is true. One McDonald's promotion had odds of 441,138,000 to 1 against winning the grand prize of $500,000. Yet there are some sweepstakes in which there are not enough entries to claim all the prizes. The heavily advertised sweepstakes often do not yield the best chances of winning.

Almost anyone can win a sweepstakes - sooner or later - if they know how to play. Only those who do not enter are certain never to win. *Remember: In any given sweepstakes, nobody has a better chance of winning than you!*

4. Getting Ready

You can't hope to be lucky. You have to prepare to be lucky.
- Timothy Dowd, New York Police Department Deputy Inspector

The first decision to make is which sweepstakes to enter. But where do you find out about them? Sweepstakes seem to be just about everywhere. In fact, we challenge you to spend twenty-four hours without encountering a sweepstakes. They are advertised on television, on the radio, in magazines and newspapers and in stores of every type.

If you are looking for sweepstakes offering specific kinds of prizes, you need to look in the appropriate places. Business magazines and business programs are ideal forums for sweepstakes offering business products. Fashion magazines and the cosmetics counters of department stores are the right places for sweepstakes offering jewelry and expensive coats as prizes. There is usually a strong affiliation between the sponsor running a sweepstakes and the type of prizes offered. When Farnam Companies of Arizona, a manufacturer of over 250 horse care products, ran a sweepstakes, it offered a horse trailer as a grand prize. Lesser prizes included Western saddles, show bridles, show blankets, and saddle blankets.

Some of the better general places to look for sweepstakes information are supermarkets, drugstores, newspapers, magazines, television and radio. Note: For television and radio sweepstakes information, you must be alert. Entry rules and addresses are given quickly. If you don't get the information the first time, you may not get it at all. As soon as you hear or see the word "sweepstakes," run for pen and paper. You might have five seconds to get what you need. If you can't get all the information, try to get the name of the sponsor. You can often hunt down the entry rules at a store location. Some television sweepstakes are advertised only on specific programs. If you watch the next showing of the program, there's a fair chance the sweepstakes ad will be repeated. VCR's loaded with a blank tape are also handy for this.

At any given time there are hundreds of open sweepstakes nationwide. We sort through all of the sweepstakes being run and report on the best ones to enter in WINNING SWEEPSTAKES NEWSLETTER. In addition to the 10-15 top rated sweepstakes, we list another 25 soon-to-close sweepstakes separately. Our readers have found this enormously helpful in choosing the best sweepstakes to enter - those with the most prizes and the best odds of winning.

If you would like subscription information and a free current issue of Winning Sweepstakes Newsletter, send a standard number 10 self-addressed, stamped envelope to:

WINNING SWEEPSTAKES NEWSLETTER
Proven Strategy Sample Offer
P.O. Box 1468
Framingham, MA 01701

Have you ever wanted to enter a sweepstakes, but ended up not getting around to it because it was too much bother? It is perfectly understandable if this has happened to you, because it's happened to almost everyone.

Take, for example, dedicated fictional sweepstakes player David Disorganized. David found a winning sweepstakes with fantastic prizes including the car he had always dreamed of. Excited about entering, he began looking around for envelopes. He couldn't find them anywhere.

"Damn, no envelopes," he thought. Then, he looked around for stamps. He couldn't find them anywhere, either. "Damn, no stamps," he thought. Then he figured that before he went to the post office and the stationery store, he could at least fill out his

3" x 5" facsimile entry forms. "Damn, no index cards," he thought, "and I'm not going to cut up little pieces of paper!!" (author's note: David was beginning to get pretty upset).

"Okay, fine," he thought to himself, "I'll just go on a few errands and get the supplies I need." So David picked up his wallet, grabbed a few dollars and headed out to his car. Of course, it wouldn't start right away. And when it did finally start he found himself in the midst of a horrible traffic jam. This did not act to lift his spirits any.

When he finally got to the stationery store, the regular clerk had just started his lunch break and David had to wait while the new boy being trained searched the entire store for a box of #10 envelopes. And when David got into his car, he realized that the boy had short-changed him. "Well, no problem," he thought, "it was an honest mistake."

When David got to the post office he had to wait in line behind a family of twelve that was very excited about their vacation to Peru and were all getting new passports. Finally, David got his stamps. Just then he realized that he had meant to get index cards while at the stationery store, so he drove back across town.

Fortunately, the regular clerk was now back from break. Now, feeling much better and getting excited again about the sweepstakes and the new car he was going to win, David headed back to his house. He sat down at a table with his supplies neatly laid out and started to write the address on the first envelope. "Damn," he yelled, "my pen's dead!!"

Needless to say, David did not win his new car or anything else from this great sweepstakes, because he never ended up entering. If he had all of the necessary supplies on hand when he began, things could have been different.

To be successful (unlike David), any hobbyist will tell you that you must be organized. This is especially true for the sweepstakes player because there are so many rules and deadlines.

If David Disorganized had had all of the necessary supplies on hand when he began, his story could have had an entirely different ending. David could have been a winner. To be successful at sweepstakes, you must be prepared. You must have all your materials in front of you, which calls for some organization. To help get organized beforehand, we suggest that you put together A SWEEPSTAKES KIT.

Assembling A Sweepstakes Kit

A sweepstakes kit is particularly important if you plan to enter sweepstakes regularly. It will save you wasted time and endless frustration as you pursue those valuable sweepstakes prizes. We suggest you maintain a kit well stocked with the following items:

- Stamps (in Rolls), Stamp Dispenser, Glue Stick. Stamps will be your most significant cost in sweepstaking. You should purchase first class stamps in rolls rather than books or sheets. Why? Detaching a single stamp from a sheet requires two or three rips. To detach a single stamp from a roll requires only one rip. For a few cents, you can purchase a stamp dispenser at your local post office.

  Now and then you are going to misaddress a stamped envelope. As long as the stamp has not been canceled, it can be salvaged. Rip off the corner of the envelope with the stamp and soak it in water for at least ten minutes. The stamp will now be free from the paper and after drying, it can be reused. To reapply the stamp to an envelope, use a glue stick.

- Envelopes. Envelopes should be purchased in two sizes: number 10 (standard business size) and any size smaller than number 10. Number 10 envelopes measure four and one eighth by nine and one half inches. You need number 10 envelopes because many sweepstakes specifically ask for number 10 envelopes. Smaller envelopes are handy because they fit into a number 10 without folding. This is particularly useful when you must send a SASE (self-addressed, stamped envelope) for game pieces and copies of official rules or winners lists.

The most common smaller envelope size is number 6 3/4. Number 6 3/4 envelopes measure three and five eighths by six and one half inches. At first glance, number 9 envelopes look just like number 10 envelopes but they are a bit smaller. Number 9 envelopes are not commonly carried by stationery stores but can be purchased inexpensively from any quick printer.

You do not need fancy colored envelopes or laid stock. Often you can get misprinted envelopes from a local printer for free - or at a nominal cost.

If you are entering a lucrative sweepstakes and want to produce as many entries as possible in a short period of time, you can purchase pre-stamped envelopes from the post office in boxes of 500. The cost of these envelopes is only about a penny more per envelope than the cost of first class postage alone.

Some entrants like the peel-off type self-adhesive envelopes sold as stationary stores. They are more expensive but easier to seal and handle.

- Address Labels. If either the "return" or "send to" address is incorrect, you can put an address label over it and save the cost of an envelope.

- Pre-addressed Labels or Return Address Stampers. Sunday newspaper supplements often carry ads for inexpensive return address labels or slightly more expensive return address stampers. These can be very handy when you would otherwise have to print your address many times. Note: Do not use either the labels or the stamper for completing qualifiers and entry forms. Most rules require that these be hand-printed.

- Postal Cards sold by the United States Post Office. Many sweepstakes now permit postcard entries. The minimum size postcard that is accepted by the U.S. Postal Service is 3-1/2" x 5". The maximum size postcard that is accepted by the U.S. Postal Service is 4-1/4" x 6".

- Three-by-Five-Inch Index Cards and Three-by-Five-Inch Pieces of Paper. Almost every sweepstakes asks for three-by-five-inch cards or pieces of paper. Please note that United States postal cards measure three and one half inches by five.

- Sponge or Envelope Sealer. Any sweepstakes contestant who values his or her tongue should keep a supply of small sponges in stock. A moist (not soaked) sponge is the fastest and easiest way to seal envelopes and affix stamps. If the sponge is much larger than two by three inches you may want to pare it down with a pair of scissors. A smaller sponge is easier to handle and is neater. Or if you prefer, most stationery stores stock simple envelope sealers for less than a dollar.

- Ballpoint Pens. It's obvious that you will need pens, but why ballpoint? Felt tip pen ink smudges when it gets wet. If your felt ink entries are mailed or delivered on a rainy day, your addresses might smudge and become unreadable. Erasable ballpoint pens are useful for correcting mistakes. Winning Sweepstakes Newsletter subscriber, Frank Tate, suggests spraying entries with Krylon Fixative (available at most art supply stores) to prevent ink smearing.

- Miniature pocket pens. You should always travel with a miniature ball point pen in one of your pockets. Lindy USA makes such a pen with a cap that measures 3-1/2" long.

You can purchase a Lindy USA pen at most stationary stores for about fifty cents. Buy half a dozen because you're bound to lose a few. You'll need this pen to complete entries on the spot at store locations. More times than not, at your local store, the pen next to the pile of entry forms is either missing or empty of ink. All the better for you, the prepared sweepstakes player.

- Magnifying Glass. It's amazing how small sweepstakes rules are sometimes printed. In fact, they are more often called "fine-print rules" than "sweepstakes rules." A magnifying glass helps to cut down on eye strain.

- Highlighter Pen. Have a highlighter on hand when you're reading fine-print rules underneath the magnifying glass. You may want to highlight important information such as the entry address and the entry deadline to make it easier to find later.

- Clipboard. A clipboard can serve as a portable desk, giving you added flexibility.

- A Piece of Red Cellophane or Plastic. Red cellophane can be used to play most decode-type game sweepstakes. Having it handy will save you the trouble of bringing the game piece to a store display for decoding. Note: Occasionally another color is required to decode game pieces. For example, green was required in a Palmolive Dishwashing Liquid game sweepstakes to match the color of the company's product.

- Post Office Box. Many sweepstakes contestants rent a post office box for receiving game pieces, winner notification letters, and any other sweepstakes-related material. Although box rental is optional, it can provide certain benefits. For example, the box will provide an extra address for those "one request per day per address" sweepstakes.

- Record or Ledger of Sweepstakes-Related Expenses. When you win a sweepstakes, taxes will take a bite out of your winnings. However, you can legitimately deduct your sweepstakes expenses from your winnings. For this reason, it is important to maintain a ledger or record of all your sweepstakes-related expenses. These expenses should include every item mentioned above, as well as the cost of a sweepstakes newsletter, and even the cost of this book.

- Calendar for Sweepstakes Deadlines. You should record the deadlines for all sweepstakes you enter on a calendar. On the same calendar you should also denote the dates that you request sweepstakes materials by mail. You will want a record if you have not received the materials requested within 30 days. Many game sweepstakes also have prize claim deadlines to which you must adhere.

- File Folder for Sweepstakes Rules. You should save a copy of the rules for each sweepstakes you enter. You'll be glad you did when you receive an affidavit that tells you that you have won a major prize but does not tell you what the prize was. If you have a copy of the rules, you'll have an idea about what you might have won. Later you can make a scrap book out of the rules of your sweepstakes winnings.

- A supply of "Receipt for Certified Mail" forms and green "Domestic Return Receipt" cards available at your local post office. Have a postal clerk show you how these two items are filled out and then save a properly completed set with your sweepstakes materials. Whenever you receive sweepstakes prize claim materials, you'll be able to fill them out immediately and not waste time waiting in line at the post office.

Once you have assembled your sweepstakes kit you will want to have a convenient and easily accessible place to keep it. Save yourself time, effort, and frustration by keeping all of your supplies in one place. Use whatever is available - desk drawer, space on a self, or even just a box - as long as you can get to it easily.

5. Evaluating Sweepstakes

The man who was born luckiest is the man who doesn't believe in luck. - Unknown

Let's assume that you have used your newly acquired sweepstakes-locating skills to uncover several current sweepstakes. Perhaps you made a visit to your local supermarket and shopping areas, or scanned your local Sunday newspaper. Your sweepstakes kit is well stocked and today is Saturday - the day you have set aside for entering sweepstakes. With several sets of fine-print rules in hand, you ask, "What strategies can I use to increase my chances of winning prizes?"

Your question is not as straightforward as it may seem. The question can actually be phrased in two ways: 1) How can I increase my chances of winning prizes in the XYZ Sweepstakes? or 2) What sweepstakes can I enter to increase my chances of winning prizes?

Too many people ask only the first question - How can they increase their chances of winning a specific sweepstakes? Some sweepstakes players attempt to devise methods to fool, beat or cheat the sweepstakes judges. We've heard of players calling on cosmic forces, attempting tricky mailing devices such as colored envelopes and using various other gimmicks that supposedly improve one's chances of winning. In some situations, such tricks may work. But for the most part, the professional judging agencies help ensure that each entry has an equal chance of winning. (We will review a few of the traditional gimmicks in more detail in Chapter 7).

The best answer to the first question is to enter often. The more entries you submit, the better your chances of winning. Of course, if the odds are 5 million to 1 against winning with a single entry, even with 10 or 100 or 1,000 entries, winning is a long shot.

The second question, though, is far more revealing and important -- Which are the best sweepstakes to enter? To illustrate, let's look at two sweepstakes (see Table 1). Given a choice between sweepstakes A and B in Table 1, which would you enter?

Table 1

	SWEEPSTAKES A	SWEEPSTAKES B
Type of sweepstakes	Random draw	Random draw
Number of prizes	30	220
Total prize value	$5,000	$40,000
Length of sweepstakes	8 months	4 weeks
Sweepstakes audience	National	Local
Advertising of sweepstakes	National magazines and product wrappers	Local store window displays

Sweepstakes B, right? It offers more prizes of more value over a shorter period of time to a smaller potential audience. Your chances of winning in Sweepstakes B are much better than your chances of winning Sweepstakes A. Sweepstakes B was a local promotion run by several Massachusetts merchants in which we won several prizes, from roller skates to recording equipment.

All sweepstakes are not created equal. Each has different prizes, rules, deadlines, advertising, numbers of prizes, values of prizes, numbers of entrants, and, not surprisingly, different odds of winning.

Because each sweepstakes is different, a major part of the art of winning is learning how to evaluate sweepstakes and determine which are the best to enter. The best sweepstakes are the ones that offer you the best chances of winning good prizes. Our winning sweepstakes strategy can best be summed up in the acronym SAFE. SAFE stands for:

- *S*elect Carefully
- *A*ct Quickly
- *F*ollow the Fine-Print Rules.
- *E*nter Often.

S-Select Carefully. This means concentrating your entries on the best sweepstakes. To win consistently, one must enter the sweepstakes with superior odds. You must weed out the losing sweepstakes from the winning ones.

A-Act Quickly. All sweepstakes have entry deadlines, and unlike your fourth-grade teacher, sponsors and judging organizations do not accept the "my cat ate my entry and that's why it's late" excuse. In fact, many of the better sweepstakes have short deadlines. Occasionally, bonus prizes are offered for early entrants. Opportunities are rarely repeated. Act quickly; always have all the necessary supplies on hand. Don't fall into the David Disorganized trap!

F-Follow the Fine-Print Rules. The most fundamental part of the winning sweepstakes strategy is following the fine-print rules.

If you don't do this, regardless of how many times you enter, you will not win. There is no greater waste of time, postage, and energy than having your entries disqualified.

When the rules are ambiguous, interpret them in the most stringent manner possible. This is, literally, playing it SAFE. This practice ensures that yours will not be part of the up to 25 percent of all entries that some judging organizations disqualify.

E-Enter Often. This is a sure-fire way to increase the probability that you will win. People who never enter sweepstakes never win. To win consistently, you must enter the better sweepstakes - and often. We recommend that all sweepstakes hobbyists set up a budget and allot a specific time for their hobby.

Hundreds, if not thousands, of sweepstakes players have successfully used the SAFE strategy to win great prizes. One of our favorite examples is a pilot who figured that he could win a Cessna airplane. The sweepstakes he entered offered a Cessna plane worth $75,000 as the grand prize. It was open only to pilots who had received their license in the last six months. The pilot reasoned that the sweeps had a limited audience and would therefore attract few entrants. So he submitted tens of thousands of entries. He was so confident of winning that he made arrangements to sell the plane before actually winning the sweepstakes. And win the sweepstakes he did!

Analyzing sweepstakes and the odds of winning need not be a cumbersome task. While it is possible to use a computer model to analyze sweepstakes characteristics, a hand calculator and a clear mind are all that is essential.

The first step in evaluating any given sweepstakes is to determine the kind of sweepstakes it is -- random draw, game or second chance. As you will soon discover, the type of sweepstakes has impact on your chances of winning.

Random Draw Sweepstakes

In random draw sweepstakes, your chances of winning are determined by the number of prizes offered and the number of eligible entries received.

Since the number of prizes offered in random draw sweepstakes is fixed, it is the number of entries that determines your odds of winning. Below is a list of factors that can reduce the number of eligible entries in random draws -- and therefore increase your chances of winning.

Factors That Can Affect the Number of Entries in Random Draw Sweepstakes

1. *Knowledge Qualifiers*. Qualifiers that require special knowledge or research reduce the number of eligible entries. In the "Gilbey's More than $100,000 Sweepstakes" each entry had to include the name of the Gilbey family crest. This information could be found only on bottles of Gilbey Gin.

2. *Television Qualifiers*. A television qualifier is one that requires the sweepstakes player to watch a television program to obtain the words necessary to make an entry eligible. These qualifiers are especially restrictive because potential entrants must a) read the sweepstakes rules in advance of the program airing, b) view the program, and c) catch the qualifier as it airs. Often these qualifiers are not repeated, so it is essential to get the qualifier on the first try. For example, to enter the "Miss America $100,000 Scholarship Sweepstakes," entrans had to watch commercials during the airing of the 1984 Miss America Pageant and listen for special phrases during American Greetings commercials. These phrases had to be written on each entry.

3. *Long Qualifiers*. When qualifiers are more than five or six words long, few entrants will bother submitting multiple entries. Many find lengthy qualifiers to be a chore to print. Imagine the

effort involved in completing a dozen entries to the "Chocolate Lovers' Sweepstakes," which had to include the following hand-printed words: "Duncan Hines Mix/Frosting/Brownies/Chocolate Chip Cookies Chocolate Lovers' Sweepstakes."

4. *Limited Sweepstakes Audiences*. Sweepstakes that are targeted to a local or regional audience attract fewer entries. The "Hood Look Under the Cap Sweepstakes," for example, was promoted only in the Northeast where Hood's products are distributed. Usually anyone in the country can enter these regional sweepstakes. The difficulty is finding out about them in the first place. This is a good reason to subscribe to a sweepstakes newsletter.

Certain types of local sweepstakes tend to be better than others. For example, the odds of winning a one-day grand opening promotion are usually quite good. The sponsors are trying to attract new customers with good prizes, and because these sweeps are difficult to enter (the entrant must visit the store that day), few people do. When the weather is bad, there will be even fewer entrants.

Often, a local store will run a sweepstakes and not leave the entry blanks readily available, requiring potential entrants to ask the clerk for forms. In these sweeps there are usually far fewer entrants than usual because many people are too shy or don't want to go through the bother of asking for an entry blank and then filling them out on the spot. These tend to be excellent sweeps for those who do enter, and we know of many who have won -- including ourselves.

5. *Duration of Sweepstakes*. Sweepstakes that are open for a short period of time attract fewer entrants. Very often store anniversary promotions are run for one week or less. Paas Easter Eggs once ran a sweepstakes that could only be entered by phone on Easter Day.

6. *Complex or Confusing Rules*. Some potential entrants become frustrated or discouraged by confusing rules and give up

on a sweepstakes. We once found a set of sweepstakes rules that detailed five different entry addresses for mail-in entries, depending on what part of the country one lived in. Entering such sweepstakes can prove a real advantage if you can decipher and follow the rules.

7. *Two-Step Entry Procedures*. Some sweepstakes require the use of official entry forms that can be requested by mail. To enter these sweepstakes one must first write away for entry forms, and once received, submit them. Not only is this process time-consuming, but it also requires added postage costs. The number of entrants goes way down.

8. *Alcohol and Tobacco Sponsored Sweepstakes*. Sweepstakes sponsored by alcohol and tobacco companies are prohibited in several states. This reduces the size of the pool of potential entrants. If you live in a qualified state, your chances of winning are better than average. (Alcohol and tobacco promotions usually also restrict entries to those eighteen years of age or older.)

9. *Print Advertising*. With one exception, sweepstakes that are heavily advertised in newspapers and magazines receive far more entries than those that receive little print advertising. The exception is that print advertisements that do not tell how to enter, do not affect the number of entries. Interestingly, television and radio advertisements do not generate many entries because they do not provide entry forms and the rules when given, are fleeting.

10. *Time of Year*. Sweepstakes attract fewer entrants between April and September, the traditional vacation period. This can be an important factor in scheduling your sweepstakes activity.

11. *Postage Rate Increases*. Every time there has been a postal rate increase, the volume of first-class mail has decreased for a few months. Eventually, everyone becomes accustomed to the new rates and the mail volume returns to its previous level.

The temporary decrease in the number of sweeps entries can improve your odds of winning and more than compensate for the increased postage cost. You should consider entering sweeps more frequently in the months following rate increases.

12. *Automatic Sweepstakes Entries*. In some sweepstakes, entries are automatically generated each time someone buys or uses the sweepstakes product. You can still enter free by mail but it is seldom worth doing so. Sharper Image recently ran a sweepstakes in which every catalog purchaser was automatically entered into their sweepstakes. Some banks run sweepstakes promoting automated teller services and automatically enter you into a sweepstakes whenever you use their ATM machine.

Specially marked coupons double as entry forms in some sweepstakes. After the coupon is processed by a coupon clearinghouse, it is returned to the sweepstakes judging company and entered into the sweeps. These are often sweepstakes to stay away from. Sweepstakes with this method of entry are attracting two audiences: coupon clippers and sweepstakes players. These sweeps typically draw twice as many entrants as other sweeps.

13. *Test Markets*. It is impossible for a sponsor to test the effect of a sweepstakes promotion without actually running the sweepstakes. Since advertising a sweepstakes is often as expensive (or more so) than the prizes, a sweepstakes sponsor will often times test a sweepstakes in one market location but not advertise it nationally. In order to have a meaningful test campaign, the complete prize structure is awarded as if the sweepstakes was promoted nationally. These sweepstakes are easier to win.

14. *Sweepstakes Prizes*. The value of the grand prize has more impact on the number of entrants than the values of all other prizes. For this reason, sweepstakes with great middle and lower prizes have fewer entrants than sweepstakes with a gigantic grand prize. Also, a prize structure full of specialized sweepstakes prizes such as camping products or hobby supplies

attracts less competition. If you are interested in a specialty sweepstakes, by all means enter.

15. *Hybrid Sweepstakes Formats*. The sweepstakes game types discussed below are occasionally combined into hybrid sweepstakes formats. Sometimes it is necessary to collect multiple game pieces (none of which are rare) in order to produce one qualified entry for a random draw sweepstakes. Like collect game sweepstakes, the more pieces that need to be collected, the fewer total entries that will be submitted.

The above factors only affect the number of entries submitted. The best sweepstakes also offer lots of prizes. There is no point in entering sweepstakes that meet all the positive criteria outlined above if there are no good prizes to be won. Keep the following tips in mind when reviewing sweepstakes prize structures:

A. *Number of Prizes*. The more prizes that a sweepstakes offers, the better your chances of winning. When looking at the number of prizes, consider only the number of valuable prizes you find desirable. The "Junior Mints Ms. Pac-Man Sweepstakes" offered 1,111 prizes. However, 1,000 of these "prizes" were "Ms. Pac-Man puffy stickers with moving eyes." Only fanatic Pac-Man collectors would be interested.

B. *Total Prize Value*. The total prize value is the combined dollar value of all the prizes. The better sweepstakes have a high total prize value. For a major national sweepstakes, the total prize value should be no less than $50,000.

In the last few years, total prize values of sweepstakes have steadily increased in order to compete for attention with the state lotteries. Million-dollar sweepstakes prizes are more common than ever before, and there are several sweepstakes that offer over $10 million.

C. *Transferable Prizes*. If you don't want to keep a prize, make sure that you can either sell it or transfer it to someone else. Sweepstakes prizes like cars and computers can usually be sold for cash.

D. *Limits on Prizes*. If you intend to submit numerous entries to a sweepstakes, be sure that you can win more than one prize. Many sweepstakes limit the number of prizes to one per person, family, or household. In most cases, should you win more than one prize, you will be awarded the most valuable.

Pay attention to who sponsors a sweepstakes because:

1) *Service industry companies frequently offer some of the best, most winnable prizes*. This particularly applies to hotels and airlines. Rather than offering tangibles (such as cars, boats and computers), they offer services that cost them very little. When an airline gives away a flight, it is really just giving away an empty seat. And since few people fly alone, the free air traveler is often accompanied by a paying one.

2) *If a company has already sponsored one great sweepstakes, then there is an excellent chance that their next sweepstakes will be great too*. This applies to local, regional and national random draws and all game sweepstakes. This is true because companies frequently repeat successful marketing programs. If you find a local sweepstakes that attracts few entries, you can bet the next promotion by the same sponsor will probably have few entries also.

It is crucial that you select your sweepstakes carefully because approximately 80% of all nationally promoted random draw sweepstakes are NOT worth entering. They simply draw too many entries in relation to the total prize value offered. You should be looking for sweepstakes that one or more of the favorable factors discussed above. It is especially important that you keep this in mind when you decide to submit multiple entries.

In general, the more difficult it is to enter a sweepstakes, the easier it is to win. Again, the best sweepstakes offer lots of valuable prizes, with relatively few entries.

How to Evaluate Local Sweepstakes

Local sweepstakes generally run for a short period of time and usually attract local entrants only. For these and other reasons, local sweepstakes are among the easiest to win sweepstakes. All local sweepstakes however, are not created equal.

Make certain that a sweepstakes that you think is local or regional is actually only local or regional. A nationwide chain might offer entry blanks in the local store but be promoting the sweepstakes nationally. Check the official rules. Often you can even save yourself the cost of postage by hand delivering your entries.

Local stores are generally not experienced advertising their promotions and local sweepstakes attract fewer entries than you might think. If you can evaluate the advertising for a sweepstakes, you can win easy and often. If you are attentive to your local radio stations and newspapers, this can easily be done.

If there is a box of entries, ask if its the only box. If the promotion has been run before, ask the manager how many entries there were last time. Ask when the sweepstakes started to get an idea how fast entries are accumulating. Mark your calendar and go back to the store two weeks after your first visit and see how many more entries have accumulated.

More tips for winning local sweepstakes:

- Attend local home, boat, bridal and flower shows. Almost every exhibitor is giving away prizes. Bring address labels or an address stamper to speed up your entry rate. Look for the shy exhibitor. This is the one with no one at his booth. The exhibitor is usually sitting in a corner reading a book. If he's offering a prize, be sure to enter because probably no one else will. The exhibitor will appreciate your attention.

- The odds of winning a one-day grand opening promotion are usually quite good. The sponsors are trying to attract new customers with good prizes, and because these sweeps are difficult to enter (the entrant must visit the store that day) few people do. When the weather is bad, there will be even fewer entrants.

- When at a store location, enter then and there. If you take entry forms home, they will probably never be filled out or even worse, filled out but not submitted.

Game Sweepstakes

The best game sweepstakes are the best sweepstakes available because their odds are fixed. No matter how many times you (or everyone else) enter, your chances of winning will not change.

Your chances of winning game sweepstakes are not based on the number of entries but rather on the ratio of winning to losing game pieces that are printed.

There is often a mysterious feeling to random draw sweepstakes - you submit an entry, and whether it wins or loses, there seems to be an almost magical force that is in control. Game pieces are tangible. They have a sense of immediacy. This is a major part of their attraction.

"Game sweepstakes" are defined as sweepstakes promotions in which the entrant participates by either scratching, collecting, matching, or decoding a game piece. Game pieces come in a variety of shapes, sizes, and colors. Most game pieces are cards. However, we have seen such unusual game piece formats as a jigsaw puzzle (in a Honda sweeps) and a mini-treasure chest filled with paper coins (in a Cap'n Crunch sweeps).

In random draw sweepstakes there are myriad factors that can affect the number of entries, and hence, your odds of winning. In all four types of game sweepstakes (decode, collect, match, and instant-win) the odds of winning are fixed. Unlike other kinds of sweepstakes, game odds are not affected by the number of competitors.

The odds of winning a collect game sweepstakes are based on the chance of finding the rare game piece. The odds of winning any of the other formats reflect the chance of winning with a "played" (scratched, decoded, or matched) game piece. With the information provided in the rules for every game, you can easily perform a complete analysis of the odds. Table 2 shows two examples of game sweepstakes. We will use these examples to show how to calculate the odds of winning.

Table 2

"Energizer Ready Cash" Game Sweepstakes
(Source: back of game card)

PRIZES	NUMBER OF PRIZES		ODDS OF WINNING
$1000 cash	20	1 in	3,750,000
$100 cash	200	1 in	375,000
$10 cash	2,000	1 in	37,500
$5 cash	10,000	1 in	7,500
$2 cash	20,000	1 in	3,750

Air Florida's "$7,000,000 Birthday Giveaway" Sweepstakes
(Source: fine-print rules)

PRIZES	NUMBER OF PRIZES
Air Florida tickets	12,000
Alamo Rent-a-Car for one day	50,000

Seascape One-Day Cruises	50,000
$5 Air Florida discounts	4,000
$10 Air Florida discounts	1,000
Total prize value:	$7,000,000
Number of game cards printed:	267,000

Computing the Odds

1. Determine the total number of prizes offered by adding the number of each prize offered.

Energizer Sweepstakes	*Air Florida Sweepstakes*
20	12,000
200	50,000
2,000	50,000
10,000	4,000
20,000	1,000
32,220	117,000

2. Determine the total prize value. The total prize value is the combined dollar value of all the prizes. For each type of prize, multiply the number of prizes offered by the value of one prize. Add these numbers together. (NOTE: You may wish to only consider the prizes you consider desirable in this calculation).

Energizer Sweepstakes

Value of Prize		*Number of Prizes*		
$1,000 cash	X	20	=	$20,000
$100 cash	X	200	=	$20,000
$10 cash	X	2,000	=	$20,000
$5 cash	X	10,000	=	$50,000
$2 cash	X	20,000	=	$40,000
		Total Prize Value	=	$150,000

The total prize value of the Air Florida Sweepstakes is provided in the fine-print rules: total prize value equals $7 million.

3. Calculate the number of game pieces printed by multiplying the number of prizes offered by the odds of winning each prize. This number, the total number of game cards printed, will be the same regardless of which prize you use in your calculations.

Energizer Sweepstakes

# PRIZES		ODDS OF WINNING		NUMBER OF GAME PIECES PRINTED
20	X	1 in 3,750,000	=	75,000,000
200	X	1 in 375,000	=	75,000,000
2000	X	1 in 37,500	=	75,000,000
10000	X	1 in 7,500	=	75,000,000
20000	X	1 in 3,750	=	75,000,000

Number of game cards printed = 75,000,000

The number of game pieces printed in the Air Florida Sweepstakes is given in the fine-print rules = 267,000.

4. Find the average value of the game pieces. (Divide the total prize value by the number of game pieces printed.)

Energizer Sweepstakes	*Air Florida Sweepstakes*
$\frac{\$150,000}{75,000,000}$ = 1/5 of 1 cent	$\frac{\$7,000,000}{267,000}$ = $26.21

5. Calculate the odds of winning with one game piece. (Divide the total number of prizes by the number of game pieces printed.)

Energizer Sweepstakes

$\frac{32{,}220}{75{,}000{,}000} = .00042$ or .042%

Air Florida Sweepstakes

$\frac{117{,}000}{267{,}000} = .438$ or 43.8%

6. Calculate the odds of winning the top prize in the sweepstakes. (Divide the total number of top prizes by the number of game pieces printed.)

   Energizer Sweepstakes: The odds are provided on the back of the game card. 1 in 3,750,000 or .000027%.

   Air Florida Sweepstakes: $\frac{12{,}000}{267{,}000} = .045$ or 4.5%

7. Using the formula below, calculate the number of game pieces you need to enter to have a 50-percent chance of winning at least one prize. Note: a comprehensive review of the probabilities formula is included in the Appendix.

   N = number of game card needed for 50% chance
   C = chance of winning with one game card

   $$N = \frac{-.30103}{\text{Log }(1-C)}$$

   Energizer Sweepstakes

   $$N = \frac{-.30103}{\text{Log }(1-.00042)} = 1{,}648$$ for any prize

   Air Florida Sweepstakes

   $$N = \frac{-.30103}{\text{Log }(1-.045)} = 15$$ for top prizes

8. By multiplying the number of game pieces requested by the probability of winning with one piece, you can compute your expected number of wins.

What It Means

In game sweepstakes you can use these numbers to compare your expected returns against your costs before you enter. If game pieces could be obtained for free, then it would always be worth obtaining the maximum number of game pieces for any sweepstakes. However, in most instances (and always by mail), the cost of obtaining a game piece is the price of two first-class postage stamps (one for your request and one for the SASE). If the value of a game piece is greater than its cost, then the sweeps is worthwhile. If the value of a game piece is less than its cost, do not write away for the game pieces, because (on average) you will be losing money. If you win, you are lucky.

As you can see, the Energizer game pieces, worth only one fifth of a cent each, were not worth writing for. The Air Florida pieces, worth over twenty dollars each, were a tremendous buy. Few sweepstakes are as lucrative as the Air Florida promotion, but many sweepstakes are well worth the postage investment.

One of the most asked questions about sweepstakes entries is "How many should I submit?" There is no magical answer. There is no number of entries that will guarantee a win. However, increasing your number of entries will absolutely increase your probability of winning. The formula in step #7 can be used to calculate the exact number of entries you need to have a 50 percent chance of a win.

It is not necessary to calculate all the above numbers for every game sweepstakes. After you have had some practice with the numbers, you will begin to develop a feel for which game pieces are worth obtaining.

When you have found a good game sweepstakes -- enter! Your only concern is that the sponsors may run out of pieces -- which does not happen often. Even when this does happen, many times the sponsor will print additional pieces. When United Airlines ran out of game pieces that offered free flights in 1980, it printed extra pieces and offered 5,000 additional prizes! If the sponsor prints additional pieces, the law requires that the odds remain unchanged.

Games are the fastest growing sweepstakes format. They are also the most fun for participants to play. But be sure to check that the pieces you write away for are worth your postage. Look for the best game piece promotions, check the odds -- and soon you will be a sweepstakes winner!

Second-Chance Sweepstakes

In game sweeps, many of the winning game pieces are unknowingly discarded. Hence, many of the prizes could go unclaimed. To ensure the integrity of the sweepstakes and that all prizes are awarded, most of the sweepstakes judging companies insist that sweeps sponsors award these unclaimed prizes in second-chance sweepstakes.

Second-chance sweepstakes are the least known about and potentially the most lucrative type of sweepstakes to enter. What's unique about second-chance sweepstakes:

- Second-chance sweepstakes are rarely promoted and are thus difficult to find out about. Sponsors get most of their advertising benefits from the original game promotion. To promote a second-chance sweepstakes is something of a paradox. A second-chance sweepstakes means no one won this prize in the game portion of the sweepstakes. In other words, entering the game portion of the sweepstakes was a waste of time.

- The rules to second-chance sweepstakes are difficult to find. Most second-chance rules are detailed only in the fine print of the game portion of a sweeps. Often the second-chance sweeps does not begin until the original promotion ends, by which time many people have lost or misplaced the rules.

And rarely will you find an official entry form for the second-chance portion of a sweepstakes.

- Inexperienced sweepstakes players do not enter second-chance sweeps because there is no declaration of what prizes are offered.

- Many second-chance sweeps have special requirements and complex rules. One V-8 sweepstakes required that losing game pieces be submitted as part of an official second-chance entry. This type of requirement can make some second-chance sweepstakes burdensome to enter.

Your chances of winning second-chance sweepstakes depend upon two factors: the number of prizes unclaimed in the game portion of the sweepstakes and the number of eligible entries received.

In the past the "second-chance" rules began with the wording, "Any unclaimed prizes ..." This was somewhat misleading because it implied that there may not be any "unclaimed prizes."

Like other types of sweepstakes, not all second-chance sweeps are created equal. Many second-chance sweepstakes are worth entering; others are not. How can you recognize which is which?

The second-chance sweepstakes of instant-win games are not particularly good to enter. Why? In instant-win, you simply scratch the card to find out if you've won. As a result, fewer than 20 percent of the prizes offered in instant-win game sweeps are available for the instant-win second-chance drawing.

It takes much more effort to play match, decode, and collect games. To win, it might be necessary for the entrant to visit a store location, or locate a decoder, or collect numerous game pieces. Few entrants go to such trouble. As a result, few prizes are claimed in the game portion of these sweepstakes.

A good rule of thumb is: The more difficult it is to play the game sweepstakes, the more prizes will be available in the second chance. For example, none of the available twenty prizes were awarded in the match game portion of Hormel's "Discover What Makes Spam!" game sweepstakes. All of the prizes were awarded to second-chance entrants. In the match, decode, and collect games, it is not uncommon for 80 to 100 percent of the prizes to be awarded in second-chance drawings.

In the case of collect game sweepstakes, the more pieces that must be collected to win, the fewer prizes that will be claimed (in the game portion), and the more prizes that will be available in the second chance. In other words, the second chance of a five-piece collect game sweepstakes is better than the second chance of a comparable two-piece collect game sweepstakes. This is because more prizes will be available in the five-piece collect game second chance.

Again, most second-chance sweepstakes are mentioned only in the fine print of the original promotion. They are run months after the original promotion. People tend to forget about them. Even when they remember, the fine-print rules are seldom at hand. This can be good for you however, since the pool of contestants is often small. So save the original rules, and pay close attention to second-chance sweepstakes. One note of caution: Many sponsors use the term "instant-win" to refer to any game sweepstakes. Examine the rules to make sure a second-chance sweepstakes exists. Some sweepstakes offer "three ways to win," described as the second and third chances. This does not mean you have a real second-chance sweeps. More often than not, this type of promotion is a random draw sweepstakes rather than an authentic second chance (from a game sweepstakes).

The wording "second-chance" is sometimes referred to bonus prizes that are offered to a particular group of entrants that include a qualifying phrase or quiz answer with each entry or enter before an early bird "bonus" deadline. "Bonus" prizes are not second-chance prizes.

Once a sweepstakes is determined to be a bona fide second chance, be sure that most, if not all, of the prizes are to be awarded. In one Gillette-sponsored game sweepstakes, the rules stated that no more than three of the prizes, if unclaimed, would be available in the second chance. Since many of the prizes were not awarded in the game sweeps, approximately 4,000 prizes, worth $400,000, were never given away.

Remember: Second-chance sweepstakes can provide excellent winning opportunities. We've entered second-chance sweepstakes in which every entry we submitted won a prize. One national judging organization official told us, "We need more second-chance sweeps entrants. Sometimes the second chances are so poorly advertised that there are not enough entrants to give all the prizes to." Don't miss out on this valuable source of sweepstakes prizes.

6. A Close-Up Look at the Fine-Print Rules

I'm a great believer in luck, and I find the more I work the more I have of it.
- Thomas Jefferson

The most important thing to do before actually entering a sweepstakes is to carefully examine the rules. As in a contract, the most vital information is often included in the fine print. It is these rules that help you determine whether you can, and whether you should, enter a given sweepstakes.

Most sweepstakes players do not bother to read sweepstakes rules closely. Sometimes you can get by just knowing the mailing address and entry deadline. Often, however, there are special rules included, and unless you read and follow them, your entries may be disqualified. Also, in the case of game sweepstakes, you can immediately determine the exact odds of winning before entering from information in the fine print.

Many sweepstakes rules are common sense. Some, however, are implied rather than stated, and others require interpretation. Sometimes even the most basic rules can mean different things to different judging organizations. Many judging firms even permit the sponsors to interpret the rules. Judging organizations report that in some sweepstakes as many as 25 percent of all entries are disqualified for not following the rules.

How then is the average sweepstakes player to know what to do? To avoid entry disqualifications, play it SAFE and follow the rules as strictly as possible.

Below is an "Official Rule" scenario, in which we have provided SAFE interpretations of the most common sweepstakes rules.

Official Rules (No Purchase Necessary)

1. Complete an Official Entry Form, or on a plain piece of three-by-five-inch paper, hand-print your name, address, and zip code, and vote for your favorite Widget color (blue or red). Mail your entry to: "Vote For Your Favorite Widget Color" Sweepstakes, P.O. Box 123, Sweeps City, NY 12345.

Explanation: The sponsor is offering two admissible types of entries - you can use either an official entry blank or a three-by-five-inch alternate. The sponsor specified "hand-print." This means exactly that. Do not type, do not hand-write, do not photocopy your entries. Also, give your complete address (the sponsor specifically called for a zip code-your entry can legitimately be disqualified without it). Do not forget to vote for your favorite Widget color, as this is a required qualifier.

2. Each entry must be accompanied by a Widget outer wrapper or a separate plain piece of three-by-five-inch paper on which you have hand-printed or typed "Widgets Work Wonderfully."

Explanation: No purchase can ever be required in a sweepstakes. This is why the rules explain that the entrant can substitute a three-by-five-inch piece of paper for the Widget wrapper. In this particular sweepstakes, the rules allow the typing of the qualifier. Unless this is specifically permitted, you should only hand-print.

3. Enter the "Vote For Your Favorite Widget Color" sweepstakes as often as you wish, but each entry must be mailed separately in a hand-addressed envelope. Entries must be postmarked by November 30, 1990. Mutilated, illegible, and mechanically reproduced entries will be disqualified. Widgets, Inc., and any authorized agent of Widgets, Inc., will not be liable for lost or stolen entries.

Explanation: The sponsor clearly states what will invalidate an entry. There is no limit on the number of entries you can submit, but each must be mailed separately, must be produced by a human hand, and must be postmarked by November 30, 1990. Note: When an entry calls for a "received by" date rather than a "postmarked by" date, you should try to mail your entries a full week beforehand. One rule that is universally enforced is the deadline. Entries received one day after the deadline are ineligible.

4. All winners will be notified by mail no later than December 31, 1990. Winners may be required to sign an affidavit of eligibility. Prize winners should allow six to eight weeks after notification for receipt of their prizes.

Explanation: Winner of major (and sometimes even minor) prizes may be required to sign an affidavit swearing that they are eligible to win a prize. This means that you have followed all the rules of the sweepstakes and are not related to anyone involved in the sweepstakes (sponsor, sponsor's promoter, judging organization, advertising agency, and so forth).

5. Winners will be determined in a random drawing conducted by A-Okay Sweepstakes Judging, Inc., an independent judging organization, whose decisions are final. All prizes will be awarded. Limit of one prize per household.

Explanation: Notice that the promotion is not begin judged by the sponsor, but rather by a judging organization. The presence of such an organization assures that the promotion will be honestly run. The sponsor has placed a limit on the number of prizes one family can win - one. So if a household were to be selected more than once, it would receive only the best of the prizes and could not receive any of the others.

6. One Grand Prize of $50,000, 5 First Prizes of $10,000, 10 Second Prizes of $1,000, and 2000 Third Prizes of one-year supply of Widgets (a $17 value). Odds of winning a prize will be *determined by the number of entries received.*

Explanation: This is a list of available prizes. From this, the entrant can determine the total prize value of the sweepstakes. For this promotion the total prize value is $144,000. In a random draw sweepstakes such as this, the odds of winning are always determined by the number of entries received. In game sweepstakes, the odds are always fixed because the number of entries is limited to the number of game pieces printed.

7. This sweepstakes is open to residents of the continental United States, eighteen years or older at time of entry, except employees of Widgets, Inc., and their advertising, judging, and promotion agencies, and the families of each. Void where prohibited or restricted by law. All federal, state, and local laws and regulations apply. Taxes, if any, are the sole responsibility of the prize winner. Prizes are not transferable or exchangeable.

Explanation: In this rule, the conditions for eligibility are clearly stated. So don't bother entering if you live in Alaska, Hawaii or Puerto Rico. Minors can only enter using a parent's name.

8. For a list of prize winners, send a separate, stamped, self-addressed envelope to: "Vote For Your Favorite Widget Color" Sweepstakes Winners List, P.O. Box 321, Sweeps City, NY 12345.

Explanation: It is possible to obtain a sweepstakes winners list for every sweepstakes. These details are generally the last outlined in the official rules. Be careful not to send winner lists requests to the entry address.

Most sweepstakes agencies are not inflexible in the interpretation of sweepstakes rules. However, some are completely inflexible. To make matters worse, some sweepstakes agencies leave rule interpretations to the sweepstakes sponsor. To assure that all your entries are qualified, it is wise to interpret sweepstakes rules in the most stringent manner possible.

And do not assume that all sweepstakes rules are as straightforward as those for the "Vote For Your Favorite Widget Color" Sweepstakes. Many rules are complex. Pepsi Cola once ran a confusing collect game sweepstakes. In the Pepsi promotion, entrants had to collect Pepsi bottle caps to spell a Pepsi slogan. The confusion arose when different Pepsi bottlers used different letters as the "rare" letter. Although the rules stated that all caps had to come from the same bottler, few players understood this requirement.

Not to be outdone, Coca-Cola sponsored the "Coke MVP Sweepstakes" (a match game sweepstakes). Here's an exact quotation from the game rules:

> Align the two footballs and the words, "Score With the Pros" on your game piece so that they are precisely under the footballs and printed words on the plastic window. If the path of the "Score with the Pros" "Touchdown Run" lines up exactly with one of the arrows pointing to one of the three listed prizes, and if the path of the "Run" is not touched or covered in whole or in part by a red dot printed on the window, you win the prize indicated by the arrow and a chance at the $50,000 Super prize!

Anyone who understands this rule deserves a prize.

Confusing rules are not your only obstacle. Sometimes amidst all the fine print you will come across some unusual or tricky rules. Here are some that we've encountered.

- Watch for tricky envelope sizes. Most rules permit envelopes "no larger than a number 10." But this is not always the case. Sometimes sponsors specify exactly what size envelope to send. Now and then the envelope is restricted to a certain size boundaries. For example, in a Mr. Clean sweepstakes the largest permissible size envelope was four and one half by seven and one half inches.

- Watch for entry restrictions. Sometimes the rules limit submissions to one entry per person. Many people foolishly ignore this. One set of rules we came across stated that all duplicate entries would be disqualified. In another sweepstakes, to discourage multiple entries, the rules stated that if an entrant won multiple prizes, he or she would receive the least valuable prize. Since many drawings are now done by computer, these rules are easier to enforce. Don't let yourself be disappointed by bringing home a T-shirt instead of a T-Bird. Check the rules out before entering.

- Watch for "hand-addressed" requirements. Although most judging organizations permit you to type or hand-print the outer envelope, one judging organization, D. L. Blair, frequently requires hand-addressed outer envelopes. In this case, be sure not to type or use address labels or stampers.

- Watch for universal disclaimers. All sweepstakes rules state, "Void where prohibited by law." Sponsors include this rule because it is impossible for them to check the legality of promotions in every town, county, and state in the country. Several states prohibit awarding live animals as prizes. Virginia prohibits the use of promotions for any products subject to federal or state excise tax, including alcohol, gasoline, and tobacco, one of Virginia's major products. To make matters more difficult, these law are constantly changing.

- Watch for entry information for second-chance sweepstakes (applicable only in game sweepstakes). Again, the fine-print rules frequently give an exclusive, one-time mention of a second-chance sweepstakes. Frequently the original rules are the only place you can find out about these lucrative promotions.

- Watch for multiple entry addresses. Sponsors sometimes use different entry addresses for the same sweepstakes in different advertisements. By measuring the volume of mail received at each address, the sponsor is able to track sweepstakes response. When you find multiple sets of entry addresses, consider them all to be correct.

The fine-print rules can offer many additional things to the sharp-eyed entrant. The rules can be used to determine the "winnability" of a sweepstakes. For instance, in game sweepstakes, the entrant can calculate the exact odds and determine whether the sweeps is worth entering. (See Chapter 5.)

Although winners lists tend to be the last item covered in the fine-print rules, they are by no means the least significant. An FTC report discussing winners lists stated that "it is essential to allow consumers to check themselves to see that prizes are awarded and to whom...[and] it is meaningful to the Commission to know the number and volume of prizes that are actually awarded."

It is not necessary to write for a winners list to find out if you have won. It is the sponsor's or judging organization's responsibility to notify you. In fact, sponsors have been known to go to great lengths to locate winners. Therefore, this should not be your primary concern in requesting a winners list. (One exception to this rule is if you have moved and have not left a forwarding address.) Winners lists are important because they provide useful information about second-chance sweepstakes. Since sponsors want to maintain interest in game sweepstakes for their entire duration, sponsors seldom disclose how many prizes are left to be claimed in the second chance.

You can use winners lists from past sweepstakes to help estimate the number of prizes that might be available in current second-chance sweepstakes. For example, an analysis of winners lists reveals that most match type sweepstakes award less than 20 percent of the total available prizes in the game portion of the sweeps.

Some sponsors specify the approximate date they would like to receive your request for a winners list. This restriction saves the sponsor the burden of storing your request. It also requires greater organization on your part. A tip to those requesting winners lists: to ensure that you send for lists at the proper time pencil in the date you wish to mail your request on the completed envelope. If you wish to know how long it takes for the judging firm to respond, put the date mailed on the SASE as well. But be patient! The judging firm must first select, confirm, compile, and print the winners list. This process sometimes takes several months.

Your primary objective is to enter and win sweepstakes. Winners lists can supplement your knowledge of the sweepstakes hobby. But beware! They cost two first-class postage stamps to obtain.

7. Entering to Win

Risks must be taken. The greatest risk in life is to take no risks at all.
-Anonymous

People who enter sweepstakes want to win. After all, why else would one bother to enter?

Every now and then we meet people who tell us they are unlucky and never win anything. Our first question to such people is, "Do you enter?" After a short pause, the reply is usually either "No" or "I entered one of those big national sweepstakes once, but I didn't win." It may seem obvious to say that "If you don't enter, you can't win," but it is the truth. You must enter to win.

Entering, however, is not always enough. If you only enter sweepstakes with big prizes and long odds, it may very well be possible to enter and never win. The people who enter sweepstakes only sporadically tend to enter the sweepstakes that are heavily advertised. These sweeps are usually the easiest to enter-sweepstakes entry forms are distributed to almost every mailbox in the country. In most cases, as we showed earlier, these are also the sweepstakes with the worst odds of winning. To win regularly, you must know which sweepstakes to enter. You must do some research, you must spend some dollars on postage and supplies, and you must enter regularly.

Tips on Entering

Sometimes you will be using official entry forms from "take one" pads or the backs of cereal boxes. More often, however, you will use alternate entry forms, three-by-five-inch pieces of paper or three-by-five-inch cards. The law requires that these alternative entry forms have the same chance of winning. Sponsors cannot require a purchase to obtain official entry forms. This would be a "consideration" and would turn the sweepstakes into an illegal lottery.

In most instances, judging organizations do not make a distinction between three-by-five-inch pieces of paper and three-by-five-inch cards-they can be used interchangeably. However, a judging organization could decide to be picky and disqualify your entries if you do not follow the letter of the rules. Our advice is to play if SAFE by interpreting rules in the most stringent manner possible. When the rules ask for paper, use a regular paper stock. When a card is asked for, use a blank index card.

Sometimes two three-by-five-inch cards are required to make up a single entry: the first card is used for your name, address, and zip code; the second is simply a qualifier. Do not fail to include the qualifier if requested. Also do not paper clip or staple your entry materials together unless the rules specify that this is to be done. The judging organizations find it easier to process the separate sheets. If an entry is bulky, print "Please Hand Cancel" on the envelope so that your entry is not damaged by automated mail handling equipment.

In most sweepstakes rules, quotation marks are used to set off qualifiers. Sometimes the qualifier is printed in capital letters. Either way, provide the qualifier exactly as it is described in the rules. If quotation marks are used in the official rules, you should use them also. And spell the name of the sponsor correctly!

Unless the rules state otherwise, all entries and entry envelopes should be hand-addressed. Although the official sweepstakes rules may request "block letters," "hand-printing," or "hand-writing", it is usually okay if you just print neatly.

Mechanically reproduced entries are not permitted. Some judging organizations have told us that "mechanically reproduced entries" can be construed to mean any entries that are not hand-addressed. Rather than risking disqualification, we recommend that, unless the rules state otherwise, all entries be hand-addressed. This is another way to play it SAFE!

Make sure that your entries are legible. Illegible printing, judging companies tell us, is one of the prime reasons for disqualification.

Unless specifically forbidden by a sweepstakes, it is a wise practice to use return address labels on your entry envelope. If your entry becomes smudged, this might provide another way for the judging organization to register it.

Submitting Entries

Like any other multi-step project, there are two ways to assemble numerous sweepstakes entries. You can either do them one at a time or use the Henry Ford method - the assembly line. The assembly-line method is considerably faster. We have found that one person can produce three times as many entries using the assembly-line method, as opposed to producing them individually. On the average, we can produce thirty to forty entries per hour using the assembly-line method, as opposed to only ten to fifteen per hour producing them individually.

The key to making an efficient assembly line is to keep your hand work to a minimum and divide the job into small, separate tasks. Here is our step-by-step assembly-line process:

1. Write your name and address on a supply of three-by-five-inch cards or pieces of paper.

2. Complete any necessary qualifiers.

3. Address the entry envelopes.

4. Stuff envelopes with entry material.

5. Sponge stamps onto envelopes (using stamps in rolls).

6. Seal envelopes with sponge or envelope sealer.

7. Mail the entries.

The assembly-line process will prove to be especially beneficial if you can get your friends and family to help. Sweepstakes playing can be an enjoyable group activity. Try to make a game out of producing your entries. If you are working alone, time yourself and try to beat your personal speed records. If you are part of a group, race your partners. Of course, be careful not to sacrifice legibility for speed. To stay fresh, don't work on any task too long.

When printing your address, abbreviate wherever possible. You can save time by using the two-letter postal state abbreviations created by the United States Postal Service and the shortened form of words such as "street," "road," and "avenue." It's a lot easier to write "MA" than it is to spell out "M-a-s-s-a-c-h-u-s-e-t-t-s." This may not seem important when producing five or six entries, but the savings in time and effort can add up.

Know how many entries you plan to submit before you enter a sweepstakes. This makes it much easier to pace yourself.

Time Savers

When you have some free time and would like to get ahead, consider pre-stamping some envelopes, or preparing three-by-five-inch cards with your name and address. You can also prepare extra self-addressed, stamped envelopes for requesting game cards and winners lists. Another potential time saver is to buy stamped envelopes from the post office -- though this is more expensive. Remember to use number 6-3/4 (or number 9) envelopes for SASE's. The smaller size envelopes do not need to be folded into the larger number 10s.

Organization is important to the successful sweepstakes player. Many of the best sweepstakes run for only a short time. You must act quickly. To do so, you will need to have your sweepstakes kit well stocked. Often with such sweepstakes, we have our entries in the mail the same day we learn about them. Don't miss out on the short-running sweepstakes -- they can prove a valuable source of sweepstakes prizes.

Entries dropped off at stores require no postage. If you intend to flood a sweepstakes, you can save many dollars in this way. Almost all sweepstakes require that mail-in entries be sent in separate envelopes.

Many people ask how many times you should enter a local store sweepstakes. We use the "dozen entry rule." Twelve entries yields a reasonable chance of winning without spending an entire afternoon filling out entries. Fill them out at the store rather than taking them home to complete later (which you would probably forget to do). If there is a rule limiting you to one entry per person, enter yourself and eleven friends. Try to get them to do the same for you (but not in the same sweepstakes)!

You can significantly improve your chances of winning the kind of local sweepstakes in which you deposit your entries into a barrel or drum. Try folding your entries into an accordion, or folding them on the diagonal before depositing them. The folds increase the contact surface area on your entries and give the judge something to grip when reaching into the drum. You can try this out for yourself by laying a stack of index cards together with one folded card in the middle. See which card takes up the greatest volume. We do not recommend this technique for mail-in entries. It's tough enough to get flat mail through the postal system!

When playing game sweepstakes, always scratch game pieces with nickels or pennies - do not use dimes or quarters.

Sometimes the opaque gray covering adheres too closely to game cards. If you use a coin with ridges on its side (such as a dime or quarter), it can mutilate a game card and disqualify a potential winner.

Most game pieces have a covered area marked "void if removed." The "void if removed" scratch-off area covers an encoded serial number that allows the sweepstakes judging agency to check the validity of winning game pieces. This helps to prevent fabrication of counterfeit cards. If your game piece is not a winner, and you are curious, feel free to scratch this area. But be careful. Scratching this spot on a winning game piece is a sure way to forfeit your prize.

Treat sweepstakes winning like any other hobby. Set aside a specific time for entering. Determine a specific sweepstakes budget. Have a place set aside to store your sweepstakes kit. *Remember: Your time is a valuable asset. Try to make the most of it.*

A Look at Popular Sweepstakes Strategies

Over the years sweepstakes players have tried an assortment of techniques to get an upper hand in random draw sweepstakes. Do not use any of these techniques with game piece requests. When requesting game pieces by mail, the best strategy is to request game pieces as quickly as possible (in case the supply of game pieces becomes exhausted). Below is a summary of some of these techniques, as well as an analysis of their effectiveness:

1. *Colored or Decorated Envelopes.* Some sweepstakes players mail their entries in brightly colored or decorated envelopes, thinking that such envelopes will stand out, and therefore have a better chance of being selected by the judges. One problem with this practice is that random draw selections are

almost always made by blindfolded judges, or computers. A second problem is that so many sweepstakes players use colored envelopes that the envelopes often do not stand out at all. One of the major national judging organizations reported that in one sweepstakes, over 30 percent of all entries used colored envelopes. Even if colored envelopes provided some advantage to sweepstakes players in the past, we suspect this edge no longer exists. And colored envelopes can cost several times the price of plain white envelopes.

2. *Oversized Envelopes*. Oversized envelopes have a larger gripping area for judges' hands to latch on to. Depending on how entry envelopes are processed, they may attract attention and command special handling. Of course, the size of the envelopes has no effect when judging companies use computer selection techniques. We have not used the larger envelopes with our sweepstakes entries, but some of our subscribers do report success with them. If you decide to use them, check the rules first to see if they are allowed. Some sweepstakes specifically request that entries be mailed in an envelope no larger than a number 10. Like colored envelopes, oversized envelopes are expensive.

3. *Mailing Patterns*. Some sweepstakes players like to spread out their random draw entries. That is, if they are going to enter a sweepstakes twenty times, they mail them a few at a time over the course of several days. This procedure may provide you with a slight edge if you are submitting many entries. Many of the judging organizations select a few names from each mailbag of entries they receive. From these entries, they can select the winners. By spreading out the mailing of your entries, you have a chance to have entries selected from more than one mailbag. This edge is slight and may not exist at all if the judging organization uses some other method to select winners.

Most sweepstakes entries are received within a few weeks after the sweepstakes is advertised. There is also a spurt of entries received right before the sweepstakes entry deadline. In general, spreading out your entries is recommended because it provides a more true random distribution for your entries. If you produce all of your entries at the start of a sweepstakes promotion, you can seal your entries and print your intended mailing date in the top right corner of the envelope next to the stamp. But don't forget to mail them!

4. *Envelope Stuffers*. Some entrants put sheets of Styrofoam inside their entry envelopes to add bulk but not weight to their entries. The added bulk supposedly makes it easier for judges to pick them. The envelope-stuffer trick might work in local drawing with inexperienced judges, but we do not believe it offers any benefit in national sweepstakes. Also, the Styrofoam sheets are not cheap, and the added bulk makes assembling entries more time consuming difficult.

Remember, the most important entry tip is to enter on time. If using colored envelopes or any of the other "tricks" makes you feel better, or will get you to enter more often, by all means do it.

Tips on Winning

Cy Young, the winningest pitcher in baseball history, lost 315 games. Reggie Jackson who hit 563 career homers and is the only player to hit 4 consecutive home runs in a World Series also struck out 2597 times, more than any other player in Major League baseball history. The best hitters make seven outs in every ten times they come to bat. Likewise, not every sweepstakes entry you submit is going to win. And when you do win, not every prize will be a home run. But if you take enough swings, the hits and the home runs will come.

When you do win in random draw sweepstakes, you may be sent an affidavit to determine and validate your eligibility. For your records, if you receive an affidavit, be sure to make photocopies.

Find out now who is most convenient notary for you. When you receive a prize claim form by mail, you sometimes have only a few days to have it notarized and postmarked. If you know in advance who is a convenient notary, you'll save a lot of wasted time searching for one later. A tip: Insurance agents, certified public accountants pharmacists and bankers are often notaries.

When you win a game sweepstakes, play it SAFE and make a photocopy of the game piece. And when you mail in the winning game piece for redemption, be certain to send it certified or registered (insured) mail. You should always request a return receipt from the post office. Then be patient -- processing takes longer than you might think.

When you receive your prize, write a thank you note to the judging organization. If winners aren't supportive, who will be? Ask that the sweepstakes agency pass along your thanks to the sponsor. In this way, your appreciation gets double exposure.

Sweepstakes winners are usually notified through first-class mail. Occasionally a judging organization will use registered mail, or even overnight mail when the sponsor wants to make the award by a certain date.

Some unscrupulous people use the telephone, claiming to be from a contest or sweepstakes awards headquarters. If a caller is trying to sell you something in connection with your having won a prize, it is certainly not a legitimate call. If you receive such a call, try to get the name and telephone number of the person calling. If it is not a legitimate operation, chances are he or she is going to be reluctant to give you this information. When a legitimate judging organization calls to notify a winner, it always follows up with a written confirmation.

Inevitably you are going to win prizes that you don't want or need. In such situations, winners often ask judging organizations to trade the unwanted prize in for cash. This is rarely done unless it is expressly provided for in the rules. A cash equivalent of a winning prize is occasionally provided in cases of real hardship. But it is important to realize that many prizes are purchased at a reduced rate, or are given free to the sweeps sponsor for their advertising value. So the amount of cash equivalent the winner could obtain will not equal the full retail value of the prize.

Huge sweepstakes winnings can affect your lifestyle. Wins that may seem small compared to your gross annual salary may more immediate financial impact than you may realize. This is true because a $2000 booty can dramatically increase your amount of disposable income. For example, if you earn $30,000 in a year, you may not have much more than $1,000 left after paying for all your living expenses. In this case, a win of $2,000 would more than double your disposable income. A $2,000 win would not triple your available spending money because you must pay taxes on the prize winnings. Prize winnings above $600 will be reported to the IRS by the sponsor.

It is a good idea to consult an accountant after a major win. Uncle Sam will want his share of your good fortune. There are, however, some things that you can do to lessen the blow. You need only pay tax on the fair market value of the item. The fair market value is the price that a willing seller not forced to sell or a willing buyer not forced to buy would pay. The fair market price is not the retail price.

For example, airline flights with blackout periods or restrictions are not as valuable as regularly priced airline tickets. If there are other major winners of the same prize in the same sweepstakes, get a copy of the winners list and find out if they sold their prize and if so, for how much. When we were called in for an audit by the IRS after winning the Air Florida sweepstakes, we were fully prepared with complete documentation for the market value of all of our prize wins. The audit session lasted no more than 5 minutes. Any time you win a large prize, do some homework to check out its fair market value. If you do not, the Internal Revenue Service will kindly assign one for you. Note that many sponsors inflate the value of prizes to make them appear more valuable.

Also, remember that you can deduct your sweepstakes-related expenses from your winnings. You cannot deduct expenses if you claim no wins. For this reason, keep a record of your expenses, including any sales receipts.

You May Have Already Won

You May Have Already Won ... maybe, but probably not. Publishers Clearing House, American Family Publishers and Reader's Digest sponsor a few of the mega-jackpot sweepstakes advertised ubiquitously on television and in your mailbox. For the return on investment aspect, these sweepstakes are often worth entering. The odds against winning a grand prize, as you might expect, are remote. However, their are many lesser prizes. Jeff's sister's brother-in-law won $250 a few years ago.

People really do win these sweepstakes. And yes, often times someone really does throw away a potential million dollar prize by not returning an entry. You should know that the odds of winning every one of the mega-prize sweepstakes are not the same. Often times, some of the mailings are mailed to relatively small segments. Should you enter? The answer is yes. Unfortunately, it is difficult or impossible to submit multiple entries because an official entry form is required to enter. Your chances of winning really are the same whether or not you buy anything.

If you are not on the mailing list for one of the mega-jackpot sweepstakes, just write and ask that you be put on. Of course, you could also get onto their mailing lists by buying a magazine.

You Have Already Won

It's possible to win sweepstakes you have never entered. And in the past, we have been of some service in this regard. If you ever receive a letter from us, like the one on the following page, we suggest that you act on it!

In 1989, Pepsi sponsored a sweepstakes call the Pepsi "Taste the Excitement" Sweepstakes. The displays for this promotion pictured 51 licenses plates, one for each state plus one for the District of Columbia. The license plate numbers were supposedly picked randomly from a range of available license plates numbers issued by each of the Registry of Motor vehicle departments. If your license plate number was pictured in the display and you filled out a prize claim form before the deadline, you would win a 1989 Pepsi Special Edition Pontiac Grand Prix SE.

Since unclaimed prizes would not be awarded, we took it upon ourselves to contact each of the 51 winners to be certain that the winners knew about and claimed their prizes. There are few things in life more fun than telling someone how to claim a free car. The process of finding out who the winners were quickly became an exercise in resourcefulness, organization and steadfastness (as we have said before, skills needed by the successful sweepstakes player).

We obtained a list of Registry of Motor Vehicle Department addresses at the library and tried telephoning each to get the name and address of the license plate owners. This turned out to be an impossible task because: 1) in about half of the states, the phone numbers for the motor vehicle departments are permanently busy and 2) even when we did get through, as you might expect, the information was not readily given.

In the end, we wrote to all 51 motor vehicle departments and requested the information by mail. After paying fees ranging from 50 cents to $8 and filling out application forms ranging from 1 to 3

LETTER TO THE WINNERS OF THE PEPSI "TASTE THE EXCITEMENT" SWEEPSTAKES

<DATE>

<WINNER>
<ADDRESS>
<CITY>, <STATE> <ZIP>

VIA CERTIFIED MAIL #: <CERT>
Reference: <STATE> License Plate Number <LICENSE>

Dear <WINNER>:

Our names are Jeffrey and Robin Sklar. We publish WINNING SWEEPSTAKES NEWSLETTER. The purpose of WINNING SWEEPSTAKES NEWSLETTER is to help people like yourself, win sweepstakes. What we are about to tell you (if you do not already know), you are going to find hard to believe.

Here goes ... In the course of publishing WINNING SWEEPSTAKES NEWSLETTER, we learned about a sweepstakes promotion (sponsored by Pepsi) in which 51 randomly pre-selected people win free cars -- but only if they found out that they had won and claimed the prizes in time. If your license plate number matches the license plate number for your state (including the District of Columbia) in the display, you win.

It has been our experience that many pre-selected sweepstakes winners do not claim their prizes. In this Pepsi sweepstakes, unclaimed cars would not be awarded and thus, go to waste. To make sure this does not happen, we have gone to some length to contact you.

Well, if you haven't already guessed, CONGRATULATIONS!!! **We believe that you are one of the 51 pre-selected grand prize winners of a FREE $18,000.00 1989 Pepsi Special Edition Pontiac Grand Prix SE automobile in the Pepsi "Taste the Excitement" Sweepstakes!** If I were you, I probably wouldn't believe it -- but it's true.

Our company has no affiliation with the sweepstakes sponsor (Pepsi) or its agencies. WINNING SWEEPSTAKES NEWSLETTER is the only publication that rates sweepstakes and provides the winning strategies for winning great prizes. Anytime we can help someone win a sweepstakes, we feel that it's our obligation to do so. That's why we've written to you.

We believe that your license plate number, <LICENSE>, correctly matches the winning plate for <STATE>. Of course, you still must comply with the other sweepstakes rules and submit your completed prize claim before the June 30, 1989 deadline. The official sweepstakes rules and a photocopy of the list of winning license plate numbers are enclosed.

To claim your prize, please carefully read the sweepstakes rules and follow the instructions precisely. We recommend that you keep photocopies of all documents and send all prize claim correspondences via Certified mail. If you do not claim your prize before June 30, 1989, you will not receive it.

We are available to assist you with any questions or concerns you might have. We are eager to hear about your reaction and of any plans you might have for the new car. Again, CONGRATULATIONS!!!

Sincerely,

Jeffrey and Robin Sklar
Publishers

pages, we obtained the names and addresses of 44 of the sweepstakes winners. The next task, notifying the winners, turned out to be far more challenging.

We didn't think any of the winners would believe us if we telephoned. We assumed that most people would question the authenticity of anyone claiming that you've already won a car. It is hard enough to convince friends and family members about sweepstakes wins, but to convince total strangers seemed farfetched.

So we decided to write to each of the winners. Put down this book for a minute and in your mind, try to draft a letter to the likely winner of a free car. If you give this some thought you'll understand the problem we encountered.

The letter (see Pepsi letter) was tinkered with by at least a dozen people before it was mailed. To add believability, with each letter we included, a copy of Winning Sweepstakes Newsletter, copies of a few newspaper clippings about Winning Sweepstakes Newsletter, a copy of the official rules, a copy of the display listing the winning license plate numbers and a prize claim form.

Each package was sent by certified mail, return receipt requested. At mailing time, we were as excited as if we had won the cars ourselves. It would have been great fun to be a fly on the wall when our packages were opened. As it turned out, most of the winners had already been notified. More people have ready access to motor vehicle records than you would think. A few charlatans even tried to get some of the winners to sign away part of their prizes in exchange for telling them how to claim the prize. Nearly all the winners we contacted were ecstatic about their good fortune. Several of the winners were driving old, beat-up cars at the time. One of the winners was a Porsche owner.

8. Winning Sweepstakes

"Ya gotta believe."

- Tug McGraw, Relief Pitcher for the 1973 New York Mets

There is a perception that all sweepstakes draw millions of entries. This is false but you would never know it from what one reads in the media. From the sponsor's perspective, the more entries that a sweepstakes draws, the more successful the sweepstakes. If a sweepstakes draws scores or hundreds of thousands (or millions) of entries, then the sponsor is likely to publicize the success of the promotion. If there are few entries, the sponsor generally keeps quiet.

In Winning Sweepstakes Newsletter, the top 10% to 15% of all sweepstakes are rated from one to four stars. Lesser sweepstakes do not receive a star rating. The top rated fixed odds, game sweepstakes can receive a rating up to four stars. However, four star rated sweepstakes are rare. We have averaged only one every seven issues since Winning Sweepstakes Newsletter has been in publication.

Random draw sweepstakes can be rated as highly as three stars. They are never rated four stars because the odds can never be guaranteed. To date, we have personally never lost a four star sweepstakes. And all of those sweepstakes have been equally available to the subscribers of Winning Sweepstakes Newsletter. More than a few times, we have been called the Babe Ruth of sweepstakes for predicting our home runs in advance of hitting them. Babe Ruth was alleged to have signalled that he was going to hit a ball over the center field fence at the 1932 All-Star game in Wrigley Field before actually doing so.

Local and regional sweepstakes typically draw from 2,000 to 75,000 entries. The high end range is much greater for national sweepstakes. Direct mail sweepstakes can draw the most entries because they are so easy to enter. After the fact, it is obvious many times when there were few entries. If you submit 7 entries and they all win watches (yes, this actually happened to us), then you can surmise that there were few entries.

In the course of publishing Winning Sweepstakes Newsletter we are frequently in contact with sweepstakes sponsors who do not have enough entries to award all the prizes! Although the sweepstakes sponsors almost always request anonymity, we factor this information into our star ratings.

Before the TWA sweepstakes win, we told all our friends and family how great the odds were and no one entered. Again before the outrageous Air Florida sweepstakes wins, we told all our friends and family how great the odds were and no one entered. By this time we were publishing our sweepstakes calculations and predictions in Winning Sweepstakes Newsletter. When we published the Beatrice Monday Night Winning Line-Up Sweepstakes, still no one believed.

Finally after years of watching us win, everyone we knew participated in the KayBee / CapriSun Free Toys Sweepstakes. In that sweepstakes, we won over $6000 worth of merchandise. In Jeff's family, his parents, brother, sister, brother-in-law, brother-in-law's mother and nearly all of our friends won hundreds to thousands of dollars each! If there was a record for the most family members winning major prizes in a single sweepstakes, we probably set it in this promotion. Before the KayBee / Capri sweepstakes was reported in Winning Sweepstakes Newsletter, only a handful of prizes were claimed. After our exclusive write-up, the winners list was over 140 pages long of computer print! To date, we've won well over 2000 career sweepstakes prizes. Here is the story of but a few of our wins in the past year ...

In the Microsoft "I Want It All" Sweepstakes June 1989), there were two ways of entering. Method one was by mail. Method two was at your local participating Microsoft computer retailer. Each local retailer nationwide awarded two $1000 Microsoft computer shopping sprees. In our local area, we surveyed several participating dealers and found that the total number of entries at each location ranged from 25 to 100. This meant that with only one entry, your chance of winning was from 1 in 12.5 to 1 in 50 depending upon the store. We won one of the $1000 shopping sprees and so told lots of Winning Sweepstakes Newsletter subscribers.

Pan Am sponsored two four star rated sweepstakes in 1989. We won a free round trip flight on Pan Am and lots of smaller prizes. Last month we won two weeks worth of free stays at Marriott Hotels and more than $1000 worth of prizes in the Visa "With Our Compliments" Sweepstakes. Last month we entered a local sweepstakes on a Tuesday. On Wednesday, the local store manager phoned to let us know that we had won a ten speed bicycle. This was timely because Robin needed one.

Unfortunately, when we received the bike a few days later, it was not in Robin's size. When we took it to the local bike shop to have it assembled, we noticed that they too were running a sweepstakes giving away a bicycle. This time it was a twelve speed Raleigh Technium racing bicycle. A few weeks after entering we received notification that we won the Raleigh bicycle also. This time we were given a choice of size.

Both local sweepstakes had only a handful of entries. The first bicycle sweepstakes we entered only twice. The second one, we entered a dozen times. Last week Robin won a pair of 1/2 carat diamond earrings worth $575. The nice part about being entered in lots of sweepstakes is that you never know what might be in the mail.

Last year our daughter Stephanie (6 months old at the time) won a 3 foot Raggedy Ann doll. If you're thinking that the whole family is lucky, forget it. She entered and lost a baby crawl contest that happened to be going on when Robin and Stephanie went shopping. The Raggedy Ann doll was awarded to one of the crawl race losers in a random drawing. Stephanie won the random drawing. There were only 3 other contestants. In many ways, this typifies many of our sweepstakes wins. The key to winning time and again is not great luck to overcome long odds but rather finding (and winning) prize competitions where the odds are excellent.

That First Win

Sweepstaking is a hobby, just as knitting and golf are hobbies. And as much as every hobbyist says they are only involved to have fun, every hobbyist has some dream or some goal in mind. The knitter's thrill is putting the last stitch into a sweater. The golfer dreams about winning the U.S. Open or perhaps finally breaking par. And for a sweepstakes player the thrill comes, of course, from winning.

To those of you who have been winning regularly in the past, you know this thrill - that great feeling when you open the notification letter, and the even better feeling when you receive the prize.

Everyday we receive letters from subscribers about their winnings. The most excited sweepstakes winners seem to be the first time winners. Experienced winners sometimes take the wins for granted. It's easy to share in the excitement of all sweepstakes winners ...

Jack Ward of Washington writes, "I am happy to report per my urging, support & help (postage, 3" x 5"s, writer's cramp) my granddaughter has won one of the ten $25,000 scholarships in the Ohio Art Company's Etch a Sketch Silver Scholarship Sweepstakes ... We are all pretty excited as I am sure you are well aware."

The family of Pennsylvania subscriber Sylvia Winkler once believed she would never win a sweepstakes. She said, "I just sat there faithfully filling out my entries, and the whole family would laugh at me. I told them, 'You won't be so damn smart when I win.'" And win she did.

D.L. Blair and Pepsi-Cola presented Sylvia with a red Jeep CJ from the Pepsi "Road to Riches" Sweepstakes. "Not one single person I knew believed sweepstakes were legitimate and that I had really won even after they saw my letter of notification. No one believed until they actually saw the jeep ... I never, never in my life expected to win anything that big. I'm thrilled to death. I just love it!"

Many entrants become discouraged after a dry spell with no wins. Norma Spinney of California had her doubts about winning sweepstakes until she recently won her first two sweepstakes prizes. She wrote us, "I had spend a lot of hours, energy and postage and was ready to hang it up when my first two wins came in. Certified letters with affidavits came from the Durabeam Match'n'Win and the Flex Million Dollar Diamond Giveaway. Several weeks later I almost fainted when I found out that my first win was 1 of 2 first prizes of $10,000 ... It is very exciting."

Some of our subscribers never experience these doubts. Sandra Flick of Tennessee won a 25 cubic foot refrigerator in the Mrs. Butterworth's 25th Anniversary Sweepstakes, and she "just knew" she was going to win. She told us, "I needed that refrigerator and I just knew I was going to win it."

People do react differently to their wins - Dee McKenney, a Washington subscriber, was on "Cloud 9" after winning a Pontiac Fiero; Georgie Oman of Michigan remained on Earth but moved forward in time, thinking it was "just like Christmas opening all those boxes" containing Black and Decker Spacemaker appliances. The common elements are that everyone is amazed and surprised and most of all, very, very excited.

That first win ... the goal of all new sweepstakes players. It doesn't matter much what that win is - whether it's a t-shirt, a $10,000 check, a cookbook or a car - it's easy to get excited. Why? Because any win, no matter how large or how small, is proof that you can win. It silences the skeptics, especially that skeptic within yourself. And perhaps the next one will be that "big win" that we all eagerly await. Winning is exciting. That feeling you get when you win was perhaps best summed up by Michigan subscriber Josie Calcari who said, "the thrill of winning is TERRIFIC!" We wish all of you success and many happy winnings.

❑ CAPRI SUN/KAY-BEE TOYS "FREE TOYS" SWEEPSTAKES

★★★★

received by: December 15, 1987
total prize value: Almost Unlimited

PRIZES: Gift certificates worth $5, $10, $15, $20, $25, $30, $40 and $50 at Kay-Bee Toy & Hobby Shops. There is no limit to the number of prizes that could be awarded. There are over 600 Kay-Bee Toy & Hobby Shops in the 50 states.

TO PLAY: This is a complex but easy to win game. Every specially marked box of Capri Sun drinks contains 10 game pieces, that is, 10 pouches of fruit drink. Each individual pouch has one of the alphabet letters printed in the lower right corner. The winning letters are C-A-P-R-I-S-U-N. Each winning letter is worth 1 point. Collect the specified number of points (see the chart below) for any letter and win the applicable gift certificate. Winning letters obtained from packages of the new Maui Punch are worth 2 points. Game letters can also be obtained by mail (see TO ENTER details below). You can mix points obtained from different flavor pouches and mail requests. It is okay to trade pouches with your friends. There is no limit to the number of prizes that one can win.

There are no rare winning letters. All "winning" letters are available in equal proportion and are randomly distributed among Capri Sun boxes and mail requests.

WINNING LETTERS	POINTS NEEDED	KAY-BEE GIFT CERTIFICATE
C	4	$ 5
A	6	$10
P	8	$15
R	10	$20
I	12	$25
S	14	$30
U	18	$40
N	22	$50

TO ENTER: <u>Option 1 (purchase necessary)</u>: Buy specially marked sweepstakes boxes of Capri Sun drink. At our local supermarket, a Capri Sun drink box with 10 pouches (that means 10 official game letters) costs $2.19. Each box has a required prize claim form printed on it. Collect the number of points needed for any of the winning letters and follow the "PRIZE CLAIM" procedure listed below. NOTE: It is best to purchase the new Capri Sun Maui drink because winning letters are worth 2 points (winning letters from other drink flavors are worth only 1 point).

<u>Option 2 (no purchase necessary)</u>: To obtain 10 Official Game Letters and a required prize claim form, send a SASE to: **Capri Sun Letter Requests, c/o MGA, P.O. Box 906, Ridgefield, CT 06877.** Requests must be received by 12-15-87. Residents of Washington State and Vermont may omit return postage stamp. **Void where taxed, restricted or prohibited by law.**

please turn to page 5

Capri Sun/Kay-Bee Toys Sweepstakes, continued from page 4

MISC.: for major prize winners list, send a SASE to:
Capri Sun Winners, P.O. Box 953, Ridgefield, CT 06877
judged by: MGA

PRIZE CLAIM: To claim your Kay-Bee gift certificate, send your winning game letters and a completed gift certificate order form to: Capri Sun offer, c/o MGA, P.O. Box 896, Ridgefield, CT 06877. Prize claim requests must be received no later than 12-31-87. Gift certificates will be mailed to you by third class mail and must be used by 3-30-88. Allow 6-8 weeks for gift certificate to be processed. Check your local telephone book for the Kay-Bee Toys and Hobby Shop nearest you or write to: Capri Sun/Kay-Bee, c/o MGA, 299 Park Avenue, 4th Floor, New York, NY 10171.

THANK YOU NOTE: When you win, please send a thank you note to: Capri Sun, Inc., 1825 South Grant Street, Suite 120, San Mateo, CA 94402 ... and be sure to write WSN about it too!

STRATEGY: Analysis by Winning Sweepstakes Newsletter:

You should make no fewer than a dozen requests for game letters so that you can accumulate a sufficient number of points to win prizes. The more game letters you obtain the more prizes you can expect to win. Remember -- trading with friends is permitted.

BY MAIL: The expected return on investment entering this sweepstakes by mail is 1256%! That is, for every dollar you invest in postage, on average, you should expect to win $12.56 ($13.56 including your original dollar) in prizes. If you can complete 40 mail requests per hour you would be profiting $221.06 per hour (on average) in prizes for your efforts.

If you make 50 mail requests (10 game letters per mail request), you would (on average) expect to win $298 in prizes at a cost of $22 in postage.

BY PURCHASE: The expected return on investment entering this sweepstakes by purchasing the new Maui Capri Sun drink is 445%. That is, for every dollar you spend on Maui Capri Sun Drink, you should expect to win (on average) $4.45 ($5.45 including your original dollar) in prizes.

If you buy 25 boxes of the new Maui drink, you would on average expect to win $298 in prizes at a cost of $54.75.

NOTES: Collect Game Sweepstakes. There is no limit on the number of game pieces that you can request. From time to time, however, sweepstakes game sponsors have been known to run out of game pieces. In this case, additional game pieces are sometimes printed ... but not always. Of course, you can always buy the sweepstakes marked boxes of the new Capri Sun Maui drink. If you have winning game letters that you cannot redeem send them to Winning Sweepstakes Newsletter by December 5 and we will find a worthy cause.

This is (by far) the most space we have ever devoted to a single sweepstakes write-up. We hope you make it worthwhile by winning lots of great prizes!

The Best Sweeps to Enter... The Experts' Way to Win!

Winning Sweepstakes

NEWSLETTER

Jeffrey and Robin Sklar • P.O. Box 1468 • Framingham, MA 01701 • Volume 8 • Number 7 • July 1989

THREE CURRENT ★★★★ SWEEPSTAKES

Great sweepstakes from Pan Am come in two's ... In last month's issue of WINNING SWEEPSTAKES NEWSLETTER, the Pan Am "50 Years to Europe" Game received a ★★★★ rating. An analysis of this instant-win game sweepstakes follows. In this issue, another Pan Am instant-win game sweepstakes, "The Corporate Jet Game" and the Buick "Match The Pro" Second Chance Sweepstakes also get ★★★★ ratings.

"There are so many good sweepstakes to choose from this month that Delbert's suffering from Toxic Option Syndrome."

The Pan Am "50 Years to Europe" Game

WINNING SWEEPSTAKES Analysis:

NUMBER	PRIZE	VALUE	ODDS
100	FIRST CLASS ROUNDTRIP TICKET	$770	1 in 11,000
500	CLIPPER CLASS ROUND TRIP TICKET	$575	1 in 2,200
50	50,000 WORLDPASS MILES	$400	1 in 22,000
2,500	ECONOMY CLASS ROUNDTRIP TICKET	$308	1 in 440
500	ONE YEAR CLIPPER CLUB MEMBERSHIP	$150	1 in 2,200
5,000	ONE CLASS ONE WAY UPGRADE *	$100	1 in 220
100,000	50% DISCOUNT OFF COMPANION TICKET *	$50	1 in 11
150,000	10% OFF COMPANION TICKET **	$20	1 in 7
100,000	ALAMO RENT-A-CAR UPGRADE **	$3	1 in 11
100,000	DOLLAR RENT-A-CAR UPGRADE **	$3	1 in 11
75,000	FREE DRINK **	$2	1 in 15
75,000	FREE MOVIE HEADSET **	$2	1 in 15

* Prize winner may claim 1000 WorldPass miles in lieu of prize.
** Prize winner may claim 500 WorldPass miles in lieu of prize.

Number of Winning Cards: 608,650
Total Prize Value (given in rules) = $10,630,000

Game Cards = (Odds of Winning any One Prize) x (# of that Prize)
Game Cards = 1,100,000

please turn to page 2

continued from page 1

Average Card Value = (Total Prize Value) / (# Game Cards)
Average Card Value = $9.66

Cost to Obtain Game Card = $0.50 for roundtrip postage
Average Expected Return on Postage Investment = 1832%

To request a copy of the official rules and a game card by mail, send a #10 stamped, hand-printed, self-addressed envelope to:

"50 Years to Europe" - Request for Game Card
P.O. Box 4870
Westbury, NY 11592

Washington state and Vermont residents may omit the return postage. Prize claim instructions are on the back of each game card. Limit of two mail-in requests per month per person, address or household. Sweepstakes is void in Puerto Rico. Limit of two prizes per month except headsets and free drinks. **The mail-in request deadline is August 15, 1989** or whenever all the game cards are distributed, whichever comes first. Game Cards may not be assigned or transferred.

Roundtrip fulfillment speed for "50 Years to Europe" game card requests has been 3-1/2 weeks. To join Pan Am's Frequent Flier WorldPass Program, call 800/348-8000.

<u>The odds of winning a free roundtrip ticket anywhere Pan Am flies (except Moscow, Leningrad and Budapest) are 1 in 440</u> ... not bad. The average value of a game card ($9.66) is almost 20 times the cost of obtaining one ($0.50).

Believe it or not ... in addition to the instant-win prizes, there will also be random drawings to award the prizes listed below. The game card is the required official entry form for the random drawings.

GRAND PRIZE DRAWINGS IN THE PAN AM "50 YEARS TO EUROPE" GAME:

1	50-Years of Unlimited Pan Am Flights for 2
50	1-Year of Unlimited Travel on Pan Am for 2

Total Prize Value for Grand Prize Drawings: $150,000

If you claim an instant-win prize, you will automatically be entered into the Grand Prize Drawings. If you are not an instant winner, you may enter the drawings by completing the entry stub and mailing it to: "50 Years to Europe - Sweepstakes Entries", Box 7170, Westbury, NY 11592. All entries must be received by September 15, 1989. The Grand Prize drawings will be held no later than October 31, 1989.

The Best Sweeps to Enter ... The Experts' Way to Win!

Winning Sweepstakes NEWSLETTER

Jeffrey and Robin Sklar • P.O. Box 1468 • Framingham, MA 01701 • Volume 8 • Number 12 • December 1989

A ★★★★ GAME SWEEPSTAKES: HOW TO ENTER AND WIN!

At this time, there are two huge game sweepstakes, the Pepsi Nintendo Holiday Game and the Marriott•Hertz Winter Invitational Game, receiving a great deal of national promotion.

Both sweepstakes games offer millions of prizes worth tens of millions of dollars. In both sweepstakes games, you can write away by mail to request free sweepstakes game pieces. The question is, should you?

To answer this question, we have provided below our exclusive Winning Sweepstakes Analysis. All of the information necessary to analyze the game sweepstakes is provided in the official rules.

"Never mind ME, Scotty - beam up my sweepstakes entry forms!"

PEPSI NINTENDO HOLIDAY GAME	Odds (1 in:)	Value per Prize	Value per Game Piece	Number of Prizes Available	Total Value of Prize
Free 2 liter of Pepsi Product	25.5	$1.49	0.0584	21,960,784	$32,721,569
$5 Coupon off Nintendo Products	1,400	$5.00	0.0036	400,000	$2,000,000
Nintendo Game Pak	23,000	$30.00	0.0013	24,348	$730,435
Broderbund U-Force	70,000	$70.00	0.0010	8,000	$560,000
Nintendo Game Boy	140,000	$90.00	0.0006	4,000	$360,000
Nintendo Action Set	140,000	$100.00	0.0007	4,000	$400,000
TOTALS			$0.0657	22,401,132	$36,772,003

NUMBER GAME PIECES PRINTED 560,000,000
AVERAGE PRIZE VALUE OF ONE GAME PIECE $0.0657

The number of game pieces printed can be calculated by multiplying the number of any prize offered by the odds of winning that prize. For example, the number of game pieces printed in the Pepsi Nintendo Holiday Game can be calculated by multiplying 140,000 (odds against

please turn to page 2

continued from page 1

winning a Nintendo Action Set) by 4,000 (the number of Nintendo Action Set prizes) = 560,000,000. This number is the same regardless of which prize you use in the calculation.

The total value of all prizes in the Pepsi Nintendo Holiday Game is $36,772,003, a huge sum. However, because 560,000,000 million game pieces were printed -- that's about two game pieces for each resident of the United States -- the "Average Prize Value of One Game Piece" is only about 6½ cents. Because each mail-in request receives two game pieces, the "Average Prize Value of One Mail-In Request" is only 13 cents.

Since the "Average Prize Value of One Mail-In Request" (13 cents) is far less than the "Cost of Obtaining One Mail-In Request" (50 cents for round trip postage), this sweepstakes is not worth entering by mail. The bottom line is that for every 50 cents you invest in postage entering the Pepsi Sweepstakes, you would expect, on average, to get back only 13 cents in prizes -- not a good deal.

If you still want to play, to receive two free Pepsi Nintendo game pieces, send a self-addressed stamped envelope to Pepsi/Nintendo Holiday Free Game Pieces, P.O. Box 8337, Young America, MN 55351-8337. Limit of two free game pieces per request per stamped envelope. Residents of Vermont and Washington state need not include return postage. All requests must be received before January 10, 1990. Game ends the earlier of January 31, 1990 or when the supply of specially marked cans or case wraps is exhausted.

MARRIOTT HERTZ WINTER INVITATIONAL GAME	Odds (1 in:)	Value per Prize	Value per Game Piece	Number of Prizes Available	Total Value of Prize
1990 Ford Thunderbird	190,000	$17,500	0.0921	50	$875,000
Marriott Resort Vacation	47,500	$3,500	0.0737	200	$700,000
American Airlines Round-Trip for Two	12,667	$1,000	0.0789	750	$750,000
Wilson Gear Effect Golf Clubs	47,500	$750	0.0158	200	$150,000
Hertz 7-Day Rental	27,143	$250	0.0092	350	$87,500
Wilson Graphite Tennis Racquet	23,750	$150	0.0063	400	$60,000
Marriott 2 for Breakfast Weekend Night	1,188	$80	0.0673	8,000	$640,000
Marriott Dinner for Two ($60 value)	1,188	$60	0.0505	8,000	$480,000
Hertz 1-Day Weekend Rental	1,188	$35	0.0295	8,000	$280,000
Marriott Lunch for Two ($30 value)	950	$30	0.0316	10,000	$300,000
American Airlines $25 Certificate	10	$25	2.5000	1,051,528	$26,288,200
Marriott $20 Off Weekend Night	10	$20	2.0000	1,051,528	$21,030,560
Hertz $20 Off Weekly Rental	10	$20	2.0000	1,051,528	$21,030,560
Hertz Upgrade	10	$20	2.0000	1,051,528	$21,030,560
Marriott $5 Certificate	19	$5	0.2632	525,764	$2,628,820
TOTALS			$9.22	4,767,826	$96,331,200

NUMBER GAME PIECES PRINTED	9,500,000
AVERAGE PRIZE VALUE OF ONE GAME PIECE	$9.22

The total value of all prizes in the Marriott•Hertz Winter Invitational Game is $96,331,200, again, a huge sum. However, only 9,500,000 million game pieces were printed -- that's about 1 Marriott•Hertz game piece for every 58 Pepsi Nintendo game pieces printed.

please turn to page 3

The Best Sweeps to Enter...The Experts' Way to Win!

Winning Sweepstakes NEWSLETTER

Jeffrey and Robin Sklar • P.O. Box 1468 • Framingham, MA 01701 • Volume 9 • Number 7 • July 1990

★★★★ FOR VISA/MARRIOTT GAME AND ★★★ FOR BUICK SECOND CHANCE

We have a new ★★★★ sweepstakes this month, the Visa "With Our Compliments Sweepstakes" (sponsored by Visa and Marriott). If you travel, plan to travel or would like to travel, this is a must enter sweepstakes. If you submit more than a half dozen entries, you will win (at the very least) valuable Marriott discount travel prizes. Of course, the more you enter, the more you win.

"Let's see, it says, to enter, print your name on a plain 3"x5" piece of papyrus."

The Visa "With Our Compliments Sweepstakes" has four different types of game cards. Each of the game cards offers the same "common" set of prizes and then offers additional prizes for the four Marriott chains: 1) Marriott® Hotels, Resorts and Suites, 2) Courtyard by Marriott®, 3) Fairfield Inn® and 4) Residence Inn®.

WHEN TO PLAY GAME SWEEPSTAKES -- A RULE OF THUMB

To determine whether or not it is worthwhile to play any game sweepstakes (aside from following our advice), divide the total prize value by the number of game cards printed. If this figure, the "Average Prize Value of One Mail-in Request", is greater than your "Cost of Obtaining One Mail-In Request" (postage), the game is worth playing. If the "Average Prize Value of One Mail-in Request", is less than your "Cost of Obtaining One Mail-In Request", do not play.

The "Average Prize Value of One Mail-In Request" for the Marriott Hotels and Resorts version is a staggering $41.14. If you find any of the prizes attractive, this sweepstakes is a fixed odds winner that is very worth entering by mail. <u>For every 50 cents you invest in round trip postage, you would on average, expect to win almost 80 times your investment</u>!

A listing of the available prizes follows. And for those interested, also included is our game analysis.

please turn to page 2

VISA/MARRIOTT GAME continued from page 1

COMMON PRIZES	# PRIZES AVAILABLE	VALUE PER PRIZE	TOTAL PRIZE VALUE	VALUE PER GAME PIECE	ODDS OF WINNING
5 Years of week-long vacations at Marriott Resorts	1	$12,900	$12,900	$0.011	1:1,172,610
A trip to the Orient	5	$10,350	$51,750	$0.044	1:235,522
Week-long vacation at any Marriott Hotel or Resort in continental U.S.	50	$1,930	$96,500	$0.016	1:23,452
3-day Getaway Package at any Marriott Resort in continental U.S.	200	$1,125	$225,000	$0.192	1:5,863
2 American Airlines $50 discount coupons	140,695	$50	$7,034,750	$6.00	1:8
Buy one dinner entree, get one free at Marriott Hotels and Resorts Restaurant	123,000	$21	$2,583,000	$2.20	1:10
Marriott Gift shop 30% discount coupon	126,869	$9	$1,141,821	$0.97	1:9
"COMMON" PRIZE TOTALS BASED ON 1,172,161 GAME CARDS (PER OFFICIAL RULES)			$11,145,721	$9.51	

MARRIOTT HOTELS AND RESORTS	# PRIZES AVAILABLE	VALUE PER PRIZE	TOTAL PRIZE VALUE	VALUE PER GAME PIECE	ODDS OF WINNING
* "Two for Breakfast" 1 Night Stay	1,000	$69	$69,000	$0.15	1:460
* Buy One Weekend Night Get One Weekend Night Free	82,802	$84	$6,955,368	$15.13	1:6
* $20 off Weekend Night	376,000	$20	$7,520,000	$16.35	1:1.2
HOTELS AND RESORTS PRIZE TOTALS BASED ON 459,802 GAME CARDS (PER OFFICIAL RULES)			$14,544,368	$31.63	

* These prizes are offered only in the Marriott Hotels and Resorts version of the Visa "With Our Compliments Sweepstakes". Similar prizes are offered in the other 3 versions of the sweepstakes.

GAME ANALYSIS SUMMARY (FOR THE MARRIOTT HOTELS AND RESORTS GAME CARD):

** 39.2% PRORATED SHARE OF "COMMON" PRIZES:	$ 4,372,117
MARRIOTT HOTELS AND RESORTS PRIZES:	$14,544,368
TOTAL PRIZE VALUE	$18,916,485
NUMBER OF GAME CARDS PRINTED:	459,802
AVERAGE PRIZE VALUE PER ENTRY	$41.14

9. Sweepstakes Promotion Agencies

"The race is not to the swift, nor the battle to the strong, either yet bread to the wise, nor yet riches to men of understanding, nor yet favor to men of skill, but time and chance happeneth to them all."
- Ecclesiastes

Most sweepstakes players view the judging organizations as merely that. However, acting as an independent judging organization is just one of the many services offered by the sweepstakes agencies. In the advertising trade, they are known as sales promotion agencies.

In the last decade the number of promotion agencies has grown from a small coterie to a burgeoning group. Currently, there are 790 promotion agencies in our database. The three factors that have led to this rapid growth are: (1) the complexity of sweepstakes legalities, (2) the high level of expertise required by sophisticated marketing techniques and (3) the boom in the number of sweepstakes sponsored.

Every state and government agency has seemingly enacted their own sweepstakes laws and regulations. In several states, promotional games are prohibited at gasoline stations. Delaware, Maine, Massachusetts, Nevada, New Jersey and Virginia prohibit them completely, and New Hampshire has placed restrictions on them.

Since the laws of Washington state regard return postage as a consideration, Washington residents can not be required to send a self-addressed stamped envelope to receive an entry form or a game card. This serves as a benefit for Washington residents as they can save money in postage. However, because of this regulation, some sponsors void their sweepstakes in Washington.

Retailers in Alabama and Hawaii must make game pieces available at store locations in case consumers do not wish to write away for them. The ink and paper used in game cards is regulated. If the game card is enclosed with food materials, it must be approved by the FDA or packaged separately. Many states have legislation governing alcohol promotions and how often sweepstakes can be run.

These laws are just a sampling of the myriad of sweepstakes laws. The complexity of sweepstakes laws and the frequency with which they are changing, have made it more difficult for sweepstakes sponsors to keep track of them. To keep sweepstakes promoters up to date, newsletters and industry associations, such as the Promotional Marketing Association of America, regularly issue updates on changes to sweepstakes laws.

In the early 60's, there was widespread corruption in the promotions of the food and gasoline retailing industries. Friends and family of the retail store owners turned up as winners. The FTC enacted regulations designed to clean up the industry. Most of these regulations applied only to the food and gasoline retail industries but are applied by many agencies to all sweepstakes promotions. Unfortunately, there are some agencies that permit sponsors to not award unclaimed game sweepstakes prizes.

Since 1980 and along with the acceptance of lotteries, there has been an easing of sweepstakes regulation. Several states, including Wisconsin, which previously had the most stringent laws, now permit virtually all types of sweepstakes. If you would like information about sweepstakes laws in your state, write to your state's attorney general office. A listing of addresses for all the state attorney generals is included in the Appendix B of this book.

What Promotion Agencies Do

- Help the sponsor select the right type of promotion - random draw sweepstakes, game sweepstakes or contest.

- Design of Sweepstakes. Judging organizations help sponsors design every aspect of their sweepstakes. They assist in writing the advertising copy and help determine what prizes and how many to award. Good promotion agencies have vast experience in predicting what customers will be attracted by and are knowledgeable about what makes a sweepstakes successful.

- Design Rules. Legal expertise is one of the primary services offered by promotion agencies. The larger promotion agencies have a staff of attorneys who keep current on sweepstakes laws. The smaller agencies maintain a liaison with attorneys who specialize in sweepstakes laws. Sweepstakes agencies help the sponsor design the rules. They know what can and cannot be done on a national, state and local level. It would be difficult, if not impossible, for sponsors to handle the legal aspect of sweepstaking on their own.

  The rules must also be sound from a promotional standpoint. Not only must all legal bases be covered, but the rules must conform to the advertising goals.

  There are also rules which are included merely to facilitate the selection process for the judges. An example is the use of 3" x 5"s. These are generally requested over full sheets of paper because they do not require unfolding. When selecting thousands of winners, this saves time and dollars.

- Select Winners. Many sponsors are unwilling to take the risk of selecting winners themselves. A "fix" would be a public embarrassment and damaging to a company's reputation. One reason for hiring a promotion agency is to assume responsibility for the integrity for a promotion. The promotion agency then acts as a type of insurance policy.

Many sweepstakes companies do not disclose their methods for selecting winners. They usually claim that this is some sort of trade secret. More likely is that they wish to maintain the mystery of how sweepstakes winners are selected.

If the number of entries is small enough, some judging companies actually throw all the entries into a large drum and draw them randomly. With larger numbers, they use various random selection techniques. Some of these involve the use of computers. Others involve selecting either a few entries from each of the many mailbags received, or all the winners from one of the mailbags. But the actual method used should not affect each entry's chance of winning. Each entry has an equal chance of winning and that is the only vital point to sweepstakes players.

- Verify Eligibility of Winners. After winners have been chosen and notified, the sweeps companies send affidavits to verify the eligibility of each of the winners. This function is similar to that of a detective agency. In fact, for large prize winners, detectives are sometimes hired to assure that there is no connection between the sponsor and the winner.

- Fulfillment of Prizes. After winners have been selected and notified, promotion agencies often provide fulfillment services. Frequently this includes ordering the prizes for the sponsor. Because the companies are often ordering prizes for many sweepstakes they know the best sources to get prizes at the best discount. This is why winners are seldom able to exchange prizes for a cash equivalent. Of course, the promotion agency is responsible for mailing prizes to winners.

Often, companies running their own sweepstakes will run promotions that require the purchase of a product. They are unaware that such "sweepstakes" are actually privately run and hence, illegal lotteries. Usually, no malice is intended by such sponsors. The sponsor is merely ignorant of sweepstakes' laws. But ignorance does not free the sponsor from responsibility and possible fines. With the expertise and experience of a promotion agency, a sponsor is more likely to avoid such mistakes.

The growth of sweepstakes has proven beneficial to the promotion agencies. They are now more numerous than ever before. The growth of judging organizations has also led to specialization. Because there are so many companies, some of them have chosen to dedicate their time to a specific field within the business. For example, some of the sweeps companies deal solely with game sweepstakes. Pre-selected winner and game sweepstakes require special mechanics to distinguish winning and losing entries.

The existence of the promotion agencies makes it easy and possible for corporations to sponsor sweepstakes. Thanks to the sweeps companies, there is a bright future for winning sweepstakes opportunities.

Following is the text of an interview Jeff conducted with Rick McCabe when he has President of Ventura Associates of New England. McCabe is now with the sales promotion agency, Mill House McCabe, Inc.

Jeff: Do you accept entries sent bulk rate or must entries be sent first class?

McCabe: We do not make a distinction whether entries are sent first class or bulk rate but most sweepstakes will limit one entry per envelope so as long as you comply with that requirement, first class or bulk rate does not make a difference.

Jeff: When not stated otherwise do you accept mechanically reproduced entries? That is xeroxed entries, or entries made by a computer?

McCabe: Yes, but only if they are not specifically prohibited by either saying no mechanically reproduced entries or if the instructions for submitting the entries does not say to hand print or write. Obviously that would be a basis for eliminating entries.

Jeff: Is it okay to send a number of entries within one large envelope?

McCabe: In most every sweepstakes we run, we specifically say in the rules, limit of one entry per envelope. So, say that you put each entry in an individual envelope and put those envelopes in a larger envelope, this would be considered as one entry.

Jeff: Can you drop entries off in person rather than mailing to a post office to save postage?

McCabe: No. If it says to mail to P.O. Box X. Then you must follow the instructions in the rules. There are sweepstakes that do provide an option for dropping off. An automobile sweepstakes at a dealer's showroom is one case. This would be an exception. This tends to be for practical reasons.

That's because our fulfillment centers and that for most judging organizations are really not set up to handle walk in traffic. The other point is that it would provide an unfair advantage to people who live close to the fulfillment center.

Jeff: Legally sweepstakes can not require a consideration, that is, a product purchase as a condition of entry. Why isn't postage also a consideration?

McCabe: That's because the sponsor of the sweepstakes does not benefit from the purchase of postage. You could even make that same argument for a print sweepstakes. When you have to buy the magazine to find out about the sweepstakes, is that not consideration? Well, say the sweepstakes is being run by Ocean Spray. Ocean Spray does not get any economic benefit from you buying the magazine.

If, RedBook was running the sweepstakes, they could not require you to buy their magazine to enter. They would need to give you a means of entry and finding out about the sweepstakes without purchasing the magazine. So, what consideration means, is that the sponsor cannot benefit economically from a transaction related to the sweepstakes.

Jeff: What is the difference between hand printing, printing and block letters?

McCabe: They really mean the same thing. What we're looking for is printed letters rather than script letters. Print writing rather than cursive writing. The rationale behind this is that we're trying to get people to write legibly. The best advice you could give to your readers is to follow the rules exactly.

Of course, some judging organization may choose to interpret that rule literally. A client of ours could also request that we interpret the rule literally. That rule is in there to communicate the concept of writing clearly.

Jeff: Does Ventura Associates accept typed outer entry envelopes?

McCabe: Yes, we have no restriction on how the envelope is addressed. As long as it reaches us. That is, it is addressed properly and its legible so that the post office can deliver it. As long as it reaches us, it is included in the drawing.

Jeff: Do you care if there is a return address or not on the carrier envelope?

McCabe: As long as the envelope reaches us, it is included in the drawing. Now I would recommend that people use a return address. Let's say for some reason the address on an entry is not legible, we will look at the envelope. We always save the envelope as a way of filling in anything that might be illegible. This is because we make every effort to award the person drawn the prize.

Using a return address could save an entry from being disqualified. Using a return address is just a good policy but it is not required.

Jeff: Regarding 3" x 5" entries, is a card acceptable when a piece of paper is requested?

McCabe: In most instances, we do not make a distinction between a 3" x 5" piece of paper and a 3" x 5" card. Sometimes we just say card because "card" is shorter than "piece of paper." So, when the length of the rules is an issue, we use "card" for brevity. Again, some judging organizations may interpret the rule very strictly so if you want to be absolutely certain, my best advice would be to comply with the rules the way they are written.

Jeff: How close to 3" x 5" must the entry measure? Is 3 1/4" x 5 1/4" okay?

McCabe: Nobody really takes a ruler or micrometer to make sure they are precisely 3" x 5". And the rationale behind it is that if we get full size 8 1/2" x 11" sheets of paper and we have to award 10,000 prizes, that's a lot of paper that has to be unfolded and the address located on this big sheet of paper. 3" x 5"s are just easier to handle. They are a smaller bulk of paper.

Jeff: Is a lined piece of paper considered plain? Sometimes the rules request a "plain" 3" x 5" piece of paper?

McCabe: In the way that we have selected winners. A lined piece of paper is considered plain. By plain we mean one that is not covered with a bunch of writing or other material that is going to obscure the address. We're really getting into the legibility issue. But again some judging organization might choose to interpret that very strictly.

If you had the option of using a plain sheet versus a lined sheet, I would recommend that you use the plain sheet. But if all you have is lined, I wouldn't worry about it. I think in 99 out of 100 cases you'll be fine.

Jeff: Would you give the same advice for colored envelopes?

McCabe: The thing about colored entries is that they do not make any difference one way or the other. Our judging procedures and I think every other companies' judging procedures, are set up so that those factors do not have any influence on the outcome of the drawing.

I've never seen anything to indicate that they do have any outcome on the drawing. So, if you always use green envelopes and that's what you have around, use green envelopes. But I would not recommend or even suggest buying green envelopes just for submitting sweepstakes entries.

Jeff: What are the top reasons for disqualification of entries?

McCabe: The biggest single reason is illegibility. The second biggest reason is the name and address being incomplete. If we're awarding 10,000 prizes, we cannot take the time and expense of looking up 3000 zip codes. If people do not use their zip code their entry is going to be disqualified.

After that, is noncompliance with the instructions. For example, if it is required to write "I Love HJJ radio" on the entry form and it's not included. Basically, this is failure to follow instructions. Sometimes we have to disqualify a winner because they moved and left no forwarding address and could not be contacted in any way.

Jeff: What about entries coming in after the deadline?

McCabe: I would say in every sweepstakes we judge, there are always some entries that come in after the deadline. They have no chance of winning. One thing that we absolutely do, is honor the deadline date because it's not fair to those people who do have their entries in by the deadline. I've seen some sweepstakes where as many as 5% of the entries come in after the deadline.

Jeff: Does it matter if the postage on the entry is affixed by a metering machine?

McCabe: As long as the entry gets there, we don't care how the envelope is addressed or stamped, etc.

Jeff: In what order do you draw winners, top prizes first or bottom prizes first?

McCabe: Grand prize is always awarded first. That way if you won a small prize, you would not be taken out of the running for a grand prize. If we did the little prizes first, it would actually be unlucky for you to win the fifth prize because it would mean that you're not in the running for the fourth, third, second and first prizes.

And even after the drawing is done, if for some reason, the grand prize winner is disqualified, perhaps this person worked for the sponsoring company, everybody would move up. We keep a record on the order on which we draw. In this case, one of the second prize winners becomes a first prize winner. One of the third prize winners becomes a second prize winner. One of the fourth prize winners moves up to third, etc.

Jeff: What happens when there is a limit of one prize per person and someone wins more than one prize?

McCabe: We do eliminate the duplicate winnings after the drawing is all done. We would always award the highest prize that you've won. If you win the first, third and fifth prizes, you would get the first prize.

Jeff: Do you need to put quotation marks on entries if quotation marks are shown in the rules?

McCabe: In most of the rules, the quotation marks are there to set off what it is you need to put on the 3" x 5". So, with

Ventura you don't need the quotation marks. But again, this could be interpreted differently by another judging organization. Of course, it doesn't hurt to include the quotation marks. You are not going to be disqualified for including them, so why not?

Jeff: How does Ventura Associates notify winners?

McCabe: Through the mail. Always first class mail. There are times where we will use registered mail. There are times because of the time factor and if the sponsor wants to make the award by a certain date, we will even use Federal Express. If we ever phoned somebody, the phone call will always be followed by written confirmation. The reason I emphasize that is that there are some unscrupulous people making calls claiming to be a contest or sweepstakes awards headquarters.

Jeff: How can one recognize which calls might not be legitimate?

McCabe: If the caller is trying to sell you something in connection with you having won a prize, that certainly is not a legitimate call. That's probably the single biggest tip. From a legitimate judging organization, you can also expect some sort of written confirmation. You could also try to get the name and phone number of the person calling and call them back. If it is not a legitimate operation, chances are they are going to be reluctant to give you their name and telephone number.

Jeff: When not stated in the rules, how often do you allow the winner to exchange a prize for a cash equivalent?

McCabe: It's very rarely done. It is sometimes done if it suits the convenience of the sponsor and the winner. And it has been done in cases of real hardship for the winner. You have to realize that many prizes are being purchased at a reduced rate or being exchanged for their advertising value. So, the amount of cash you could get, if you had the option to get cash, would not be the full retail value of the prize.

Jeff: In many sweepstakes, there are several P.O. boxes to collect entries for the same sweepstakes. Why do sponsors do that?

McCabe: The most common reason is that sponsors want to keep track of how many entries are coming from different media. A sponsor may want to know how many people are entering from supermarket "take-one" displays versus how many are entering through magazine adds versus how many are entering from newspaper ads.

Following is the text of an interview Jeff conducted with Ronald Smiley, President of New York based Smiley Promotions, Inc. Smiley Promotions, Inc. creates promotions for Ford, Coca Cola, Max Factor, Cosmopolitan and many of the Fortune 500 Companies.

Jeff: When not stated in the rules, are mechanically reproduced entries accepted?

Smiley: When not stated, yes, we accept them.

Jeff: Is it alright to send entries in one large envelope, put postage on that envelope and put other envelopes with entries inside?

Smiley: No.

Jeff: When the rules state printed, rather than hand printed, is typed okay?

Smiley: Sure, yes.

Jeff: Why do you request a 3" x 5" piece of paper or card? What is the rationale behind it?

Smiley: That is a very good question. The answer I got 20 years ago when I was working for an agency is most people, consumers, do not use #10 envelopes, they use smaller envelopes. The reason we say 3" x 5" piece of paper is that it is easy to cut out and easy to handle and just a comfortable size. We get people writing us saying, I'm sorry my whole family entered on 3 1/8" x 5" are our entries invalid?

Jeff: Well, what is your answer?

Smiley: We give them leeway, an 1/8th of an inch. We won't accept something 4" x 9". It is not fair to the other entries.

Jeff: Is a card okay when paper is requested and visa versa?

Smiley: We accept it.

Jeff: When the rules say a "plain piece of paper," is lined or colored paper okay?

Smiley: Yes.

Jeff: Is hand writing okay, cursive style hand writing, when hand printing is requested?

Smiley: No.

Jeff: Is the main reason just legibility?

Smiley: Yes.

Jeff: What would you say are the most common reasons for disqualification of entries?

Smiley: Not giving the full address and not filling in the entry form correctly. A lot of people will just put S. Smith and they should write their full name. Our rules say write you full name and address. It means your first name not abbreviated.

Jeff: When someone wins you want to know who's won ...

Smiley: That's right, it is important because regulations require that when you randomly draw a winner, you must send it to their legal name. If the legal name happens to be an initial that's okay. For large prize winners, we will verify the name. For minor prizes, we don't bother with the paper work. If it is the last prize in the structure we will just send it out.

Jeff: When there are quote marks around your qualifiers, do the quote marks themselves need to be included on the facsimile entry?

Smiley: We do not require them.

Jeff: If the qualifier is capitalized or does upper and lower case matter?

Smiley: Yes. We usually say upper case and we will disqualify an entry if it isn't.

Jeff: What is the highest percentage of disqualification seen in one of your sweepstakes?

Smiley: In a single sweepstakes, probably 10%.

Jeff: In many sweepstakes there are several different P.O. Boxes for entrants to send entries, what is the reason for that?

Smiley: Primarily because it is to costly to separate mail for the sponsor. It is a lot more economical to have separate P.O. boxes for your entries or sometimes to obtain a UPC Number or for a winners list or for the state of Washington which still has a regulation saying that entrants don't have to put on a postage stamp. Primarily because it is more economical to do it.

Jeff: Is it okay to use a postage metering machine?

Smiley: Yes.

Jeff: Can the outer envelope be typed?

Smiley: Yes.

Jeff: Rubber stamped or return address label affixed?

Smiley: Yes. Unless we have something in the rules prohibiting it.

Jeff: Does the address have to be exact on the envelope? For example, if it say California, and they put CA on the outer envelope

Smiley: As long as we receive it, it is okay.

Jeff: What you are saying is that it really doesn't matter what you do with the outer envelope.

Smiley: That's correct.

Jeff: On the inside, are abbreviations acceptable for street addresses and all?

Smiley: No. Well to this extent, if we cannot recognize it, if we don't deem that it can be received in the mail we will disqualify it.

Jeff: Would you say overstuffing of envelopes, using oversized or colored envelopes give entrants an advantage, disadvantage or no factor?

Smiley: It really depends on how you draw. If you draw by hand, I think it could. We do not draw by hand. I mean there is a person there but the way we do it, it falls out of a container.

Jeff: How do you typically select a winner to a sweepstakes?

Smiley: We have a good idea on the amount of mail which will come in and because of our years of experience, we know when it will peak and die. We will pull an Nth amount every week and put it in the winners bin so that whenever you enter a sweepstakes, you will have an equal chance of winning. When there is more mail we select more for the winners bins. To give everyone an even chance we draw every batch of mail that comes in. Another reason why entries are void people do not pay attention to the date entries must be postmarked and received.

Jeff: Entries are received after the deadline?

Smiley: That's right. We get an enormous amount in the mail.

Jeff: What is the largest number of entries you have received after the deadline?

Smiley: We have run programs where we had 50-60,000 entries after the deadline.

Jeff: What would you say is the most and fewest amount of entries you have seem in a sweepstakes?

Smiley: 6,000,000 entries for the high. We do a lot of restricted sweepstakes we once had a trade sweepstakes that drew only 3 responses. We had 12 prizes.

Jeff: We have seen sweepstakes where every entry submitted was a winner because there were so few entries.

Smiley: In general, a lot of clients do not want to reveal the numbers received. One of the first questions they ask of us is how many entries are they going to get? It is a great ego booster to the sponsor to know that many people will be paying attention to their ad and product. Some advertisers will drop out of sweepstakes because they run an ad in 5 magazines and get 30,000 or 500,000 responses and ask, "what happened to the 50 million?" My answer is, do you think everyone will respond to your ad? I ask why do you advertise at all? It does not make any sense and people feel that a sweepstakes ad will pull a response from everyone that looks at it.

Jeff: After you conduct your drawings, how do you typically notify winners?

Smiley: Depending upon the value of the prize we will send out an affidavit of eligibility if the legitimate retail value of the prize is $100 or more. Depending upon the nature of the prize by first class mail. Sometimes by express mail or certified mail. We send smaller prizes straight out with a letter of congratulations.

Jeff: How long after the sweepstakes deadline do you typically run the drawing?

Smiley: Usually within 60 to 90 days.

Jeff: What do you think of sweepstakes where the entrant is asked to pay a processing fee to claim their prize?

Smiley: I don't particularly like the way it is done. It gives the inference of being illegitimate. I don't like it. There have been cases where the attorney general has gotten after these people.

Jeff: When not stated in the rules, how often do you allow a winner to exchange a prize for a cash equivalent?

Smiley: If not stated in the rules, it is really up to the sponsor.

Jeff: So if the sponsor allows it, it is okay?

Smiley: Yes.

Jeff: A disabled subscriber wants to know if he could type entries when hand-printing is requested if he could prove or demonstrate that he can not write?

Smiley: In such a case, it would be the judge's discretion to allow typed entries, we would.

Jeff: What is your definition of the continental US? Do you include Alaska?

Smiley: When we say continental we mean the 48 states, if we want to include Alaska we say continental and Alaska.

Jeff: What is your definition of immediate family in relationship to the sponsors?

Smiley: We consider the household.

Jeff: So if a family member is not living with the household, he or she is qualified for the sweepstakes?

Smiley: Right.

Jeff: Are sweepstakes open in the US necessarily open to APO, FPO, military addresses?

Smiley: Yes.

Jeff: Are more prizes awarded in the game portion or the second chance portion of the sweepstakes?

Smiley: Second Chance Portion. It depends, it could reach 90% in the second chance. That is why people should take advantage of the second chance because there are so many winners.

Jeff: Do you often receive thank you notes from winners?

Smiley: Yes.

Jeff: Do winners usually direct them to you or to the sponsor?

Smiley: To us. This is interesting because winners probably do not know who to send them to at the sponsor the vast majority of the time. And our programs pull a lot of thank you notes. I think people like you are nice enough to tell your readers to say thank you when they win a prize. But we get a lot of thank you notes, especially with major prizes. Whether it is a prize worth a lot of bucks or not, I would say that at least 90% of the time we get notes.

Jeff: Do you pass those along to the sponsors?

Smiley: Yes we do.

Jeff: How do you think lotteries have affected the popularity of sweepstakes?

Smiley: Lotteries create more excitement about entering sweepstakes. In fact, in the last few years consumers have been writing to us saying why aren't some companies running sweepstakes. We love them. Consumers like sweepstakes. Sweepstakes are great for the sponsors because they give a brand impression.

Our company has introduced new, innovative prizes like free house cleaning for a year, free gasoline for your car for 1-year, free air transportation for life. Those are fantastic prizes. In one sweepstakes that we are doing now, the prize is free hair salon, once a week for the rest of your life.

10. Contests

Chance favors the prepared mind. - Louis Pasteur

Only one in every ten prize promotions run today is a contest. The decreasing popularity of contests is due in part to the increasing popularity of sweepstakes. Sweepstakes are less expensive to run and easier to judge, and they appeal to a wider audience. On the average, contests cost over one hundred times as much to judge per entry as sweepstakes. This number is not as staggering as it might appear at first glance however, as contests receive far fewer entries. While anyone capable of filling out his or her name, address, and zip code on a three-by-five-inch card can enter a sweepstakes, most people do not feel confident in their ability to create the jingles, slogans, or recipes necessary to win contests. But it does point to the problems associated with running contests.

Advantages for Sponsors

Despite the decline in the number of contests run, there are still many contests available, more than any one person has the time to enter. Whatever your talent-writing, cooking, photography -- you should be able to find enough contests to keep yourself occupied. Contests still have many advantages for sponsors. They can increase sales, generate new slogans, and encourage entrants to become involved with the product. Also, sponsors may use contest entries as testimonials for their product. Often contest rules require a purchase for entering, which directly increases sales. Contestants, in buying the product, may even become new customers. Even where contest rules do not require the purchase of a product, a purchase may be essential to complete it successfully. It is far easier, for example to create a recipe using a specific product if you know what the product looks and tastes like.

Contests can also generate a great deal of publicity, which is often the whole point of the promotion. A Pennsylvania radio station, WSAN, for example, offered a mobile home to whoever could sit on their roadside billboard for the longest time. The station received 600,000 entries, and attracted national publicity, including a short article in Time magazine. Harry's Bar and American Grill in Los Angeles runs an annual imitation Hemingway writing competition offering transportation to and a meal at Harry's Bar and Grill in Italy. The competition receives worldwide attention each year.

In 1987, Hebrew National received 12,500 entries for a contest seeking usable ad campaigns. The winning entry pictured a model with the headline "There's more fat on her than on our salami." The winner, Lisa Levy, an art director from New York, received $83,000. The contest boosted Hebrew National's sales by 20%.

Tips for Winning Contests

There are several basic reasons a contest entry can end up a loser. It may not follow all the rules completely. It might be unoriginal. It may show little understanding of the product. It may be illegible. It may be inappropriate. Even when your entry follows all the requirements exactly, you need to go one step beyond. This "one step" is the originality, the imagination you add to your entry to distinguish it from the rest. It is not easy to make your entry stand out from hundreds or thousands of others, but you must do it to win.

Follow the Rules

No matter how terrific your entry is, it will certainly not win if it does not meet all the requirements set in the rules. Because contests tend to be more complicated than sweepstakes, as many as 20 to 40 percent of all entries are disqualified. Do not fall into this trap. If you are going to spend the time and put in the effort necessary to submit an entry, make sure it at least gets judged.

Include any qualifier requested. Type the entry if typing is required; hand-print the entry if hand-printing is required. Always make every effort to write legibly. If an entry is too difficult for a judge to read, he or she probably will not make the effort. If the rules call for a three-by-five-inch card, do not use a four-by-six-inch card. Use common sense and follow the rules exactly.

Assuming that you have followed the rules to the letter, the next step to winning is to make sure that your entry is good enough to win. In word contests, be sure you have some good reference works handy. A thesaurus, a dictionary, a rhyming dictionary, a book of homonyms, a crossword puzzle dictionary, an atlas, an almanac, and a book of quotations can all prove useful in creating original entries. Do not be afraid to use your own ideas. After all, this is what originality really means. Keep a notebook of clever slogans, ideas, and thoughts. You might come up with something great that does not fit the particular contest you are working on, but that might be perfect for a contest you encounter later on.

In entering contests, keep copies of all the entries you submit. This will help you to compare winning entries with losing entries, and will give you a good idea of what the judges are looking for. And sometimes old entries can be changed or updated to fit new contests. Because winning entries are rarely published, if you have made several submissions to the same contest you may not know which entry was selected if you win. Because of this, it is a good idea to "key" your entries. Submit each entry with a different version of your name (for example, change your middle initial), and keep track of which name went with each entry.

Enter contests in which you have the necessary skill to create a successful entry. If you don't write well, fiction contests are probably not for you. Don't enter photography contests if you tend to chop off people's heads in photographs. If you burn scrambled eggs, you are not likely to win a cooking contest. Nevertheless, you don't need to be a writer, a photographer, or a cook to win such contests. In fact, professional status will often disqualify you. Usually you must be an amateur to win.

In working on an entry, try to put yourself in the place of a judge. Imagine what he or she is looking for. In a recent national contest sponsored by a network television program, one of the 20,000 entries was a videotape. And that entry was one of two winners. It did something that made it stick out. And that is what attracts a judge's attention.

Ask yourself what besides originality the judge might be looking for. Perhaps he or she would like to see an understanding of the product. One is not going to win a Turtle Wax contest if one thinks that the wax is used for cleaning shelled reptiles. Know how to use the product and what its advantages are.

Find new uses for already established products. Traditionally, baby oil was used on babies. Use in sun tanning came later. If you can think of a new use for a product along those lines, you will increase your chances of winning tremendously. New ideas are, after all, much of the motivation for running contests.

Pay particular attention to your own first impression of a product. If you can convey the first good feeling you had about a product, it will improve your entry. If the sponsors are looking for a new advertising campaign, they will want something that will appeal to new customers.

Make your entry fun to read, and it will be fun to judge.

Types of Contests

"IN TWENTY-FIVE WORDS OR LESS"

The two most important things you need to be successful in "twenty-five words or less" contests are the right supplies and the necessary ability. The supplies you will need will include, as we mentioned previously, a good dictionary and thesaurus, a rhyming dictionary, a dictionary of slang, and any other reference books that might be helpful.

Once you have the necessary supples, you are ready to concentrate on writing your entry. Start by listing every word and phrase that comes to mind when thinking of the product. Focus on things that make this product different from its competitors. You may find it helpful to buy the product first and use it. In fact, you may find that when your entry is about a product you have been using all along, it comes out much better.

Look at the product's advertising and see what the sponsor emphasizes as its virtues and benefits. Read the box or label. Think like an advertising executive in adding to your list of words and phrases.

When you have your list, use your reference works to create an exhaustive list of word alternatives to play with. Before you begin writing, you should try to keep in mind the five general things that the judges are looking for.

1. *Appropriateness to Subject.* It is vital that your entry be appropriate. Your entry should be specific enough that it clearly applies to this product daily.

2. *Sincerity.* Do not make wild, exaggerated statements about the product that you obviously do not mean. Be honest, and mean what you say. It will show in your entry. If you do not like a sponsor's product, perhaps you should skip that particular contest. You probably will not enjoy what you are writing and will not sound sincere.

3. *Originality.* Say more than just the obvious. There are so many entries in contests that yours will barely be glanced at if it does not do or say something different.

4. *Clarity.* Your entries should be descriptive. The judges should have a clear mental picture of what you are saying after one reading. Avoid being too subtle. You do not want to make a joke so undecipherable that the judge will not understand it. Be straightforward and clear.

5. *Creative Use of Language.* A great thing about the English language, as varied and inconsistent as it may be, is that it offers a wide variety of ways to play with words. Do consider the following techniques and use them in your repertoire.

- *Puns*. Punning can be an effective way of creating a clever entry. Use of homonyms and words with two meanings can make an otherwise mediocre entry stand out. However, keep your puns simple; one that is too complex may be completely missed by the judges. Puns have been used in the past to create such successful slogans as IBM's "We're Your Type."

- *Metaphor*. A metaphor is a figure of speech in which two dissimilar things are compared. A simile is a kind of metaphor is which either the word "like" or the word "as" is used. "He eats like a pig" is a simile; "he is a pig" is a metaphor. Tastefully used, a metaphor can impress judges. The important thing is to be consistent with the metaphor throughout the entry. If you start a comparison in line one of the entry, continue it until the end. Do not mix metaphors.

- *Personification*. Today's advertising is loaded with this technique-the talking tub of Parkay margarine, the Fruit of the Loom guys, and so forth. If you can successfully attribute positive human characteristics to a sponsor's product, you may be able to capture the judge's attention.

- *Contrast*. One of Mae West's most famous quips was, "It's not the men in my life, it's the life in my men." One effective way of creating a good entry is to take a statement, then invert it. This form is used extensively in advertising today. One example is Pan Am's slogan, "We fly the world the way the world wants to fly."

- *Repetition*. The technique of repeating a phrase, as in Hellman's slogan, "Bring out the Hellman's and bring out the best," can also be highly effective.

- *Alliteration*. This is the stringing together of two or more words that start with the same sound. Alliteration can prove an effective way of making a catchy phrase. However, do be careful with it. Gerber's slogan, "Babies are our business," is a successful use of alliteration, but this technique can be annoying if improperly used. Extended tongue-twisters, such as "Peter Piper picked a peck of pickled peppers," do not make great slogans.

- *Rhyming*. When the rules ask you to complete a statement such as "I love __________ because ..." most people will write a short statement in prose praising the product. In this case a short poem might stand out and impress the judges. But beware of being too "cute" by forcing a rhyme in such a way the your thought is poorly phrased. Also, check the rules to make sure that the sponsor hasn't specifically asked for prose.

- *Humor*. Imagine being a judge of a contest, reading entry after entry. After reading hundreds of them, even the cleverest might start to sound boring. A strong humorous entry might just shake up that bored judge and give him or her a healthy laugh. But beware -- humor is not always appropriate.

There are various other techniques you can try. For example, you can play around with the spelling of words. Some words have syllables that can create a special effect, such as the National Basketball Association's slogan, "FANtastic," or Ore-Ida's slogan, "Ore-Ida is alrighta." Acronyms can also be used successfully.

An important thing to remember in this type of contest is the word limit of twenty-five words. When the rules say "complete this sentence in twenty-five words or less," they do not mean twenty-six words. They also usually mean one sentence, not two. You will be disappointed if you exceed the limit established.

A few general tips in these contests -- many times the number of words in your entry can be reduced by changing a passive verb to an active verb, or by eliminating conjunctions like "and," which often can be replaced by a comma or a dash. As you cannot know how the judges will count contractions, it is a good idea to count them as two words. If you have a good idea, don't give up because you can't phrase it properly. Play with the idea to make it fit.

"NAMING" CONTESTS

In "naming" contests, the object is to find words that fit the image the company is trying to create for the product. Look at the names executives in the car industry have given their vehicles: Pinto (a small family car), Caravan (a car/van), Century (a durable, family car), Civic (a savings car), Thunderbird and Firebird (sporty cars). Look for words or phrases that are apt. Also, don't be afraid to create new words. You can sometimes come up with a winner by combining two descriptive words, as in "Bisquick"-a biscuit mix that is quick to prepare.

JINGLE AND LIMERICK CONTESTS

Here, rhyme and meter are all-important. Make sure that your words actually do rhyme. Before submitting your entry, read it out loud to make sure it flows metrically. One important point to keep in mind - if you don't mention the sponsor's product at the opening, do so in the last line. The product emphasis should always occur either at the beginning or at the end of the entry.

RECIPE CONTESTS

Winners of recipe contests contend that you don't have to be a gourmet cook, even an exceptionally good cook, to be a winner. All you have to do is impress the judges. Here are a few guidelines you can follow that will improve your chances.

- *Clarity*. This applies to both content and appearance. Your recipe should be written (or typed) neatly. As with other contests, judges of recipe contests tend to disregard messy entries. If you got sauce over your entry while testing the recipe, copy it over. Judges receive too many entries to have to strain just to read them. So, make your entry neat and easy to read. Any directions should be easy to follow. There should be no ambiguity. Any two people who pick up your recipe should be able to prepare it the same way. Instructions should be simple and complete, and should follow step by step. Measurements should be exact. "A couple of handfuls" may be precise enough for you, but it is not precise enough for the judges. Give everything in exact, standard measurements. When listing the sponsor's product, write it out prominently -- either all in capitals, underlined, or in a different color ink.

- *Creativity*. Make your entry different. If you enter a cookie contest, do not copy the recipe for Toll House Cookies off the back of a bag of Nestle chocolate morsels, adding a little extra vanilla. Do feel free, however, to use such standard recipes as a base for your own creations. If you begin with the Toll House recipe, add ingredients that substantially change the recipe. In many recipes, replacing a liquid ingredient with Dr. Pepper or Coca-Cola will completely change its taste. Adding crushed Heath bars is another way to change a recipe. Don't be afraid to experiment.

Try out your recipes on someone before entering them - perhaps on your family. But make sure they will be honest with you. (Tell them if they say they like it you'll make it all the time -- that should keep them from sparing your feelings. Most of the time, they'll be more worried about their stomachs.)

Be generous with the sponsor's product. Most winning entries use more than the required minimum amount. Often the sponsor is looking for recipes to put on their packages. They would prefer recipes that use an entire box of the product rather than just a couple of teaspoons. The more important their product is to your creation, the more attention the judges are likely to give your recipe.

- *Appearance*. There is more to food than the way it tastes. Not only must your recipe taste good, but it must look appealing and smell good as well. If necessary, add a garnish to help make your entry more attractive.

  Your recipe should be economical and easy to prepare. No judge is looking for a recipe with ingredients that cost forty-five dollars for two servings. After all, it's not hard to make lobster or caviar taste good. Also, be careful not to choose ingredients that are exotic or hard to find. The judges should be able to obtain the ingredients in your recipe easily.

  Last, although you might think it a small matter, your creation's title is important. Give your recipe a name that will help draw the judges' attention to it. If you have trouble coming up with a title, list words that are associated with either the sponsor's product or an important ingredient. Then play around with them and try to come up with something creative, original, and colorful. Consider using a subtitle as well, such as "Chewy and Gooey Chocolate Chip Cookies-the best you'll ever taste." It's simple and direct.

PHOTOGRAPHY CONTESTS

You do not need to be a camera enthusiast to take a good picture. Of course, it helps if you know how to focus a camera, but with today's technology you barely even have to know that. In most contests, professionals are not allowed, so your amateur status is not an obstacle-in fact, it's a prerequisite. If you have a good eye for making an appealing picture, you have a good chance at success.

In the "open" contests, what you shoot is entirely up to you. In some contests you will have to capture a certain mood or theme. Take a picture that is appropriate to the theme and sponsor. You would probably not want to take a picture of the Boston Herald building for a Boston Globe photography contest.

It would help to always have your camera ready -- you never know when you will see the "right" scene. And take many pictures. Often you can submit as many as you want. Even if you cannot, the more pictures you have the more you can choose from. Your pictures will generally be judged on both their technical merit and their content. Here your photographic prowess will matter.

In contests in which you must depict the sponsor's product, the emphasis is on appeal to the eye. Try to display the product prominently and make it look fun. Judging will be based on the clarity and the content of the photograph. Make the picture look both sincere and interesting. A typical contest might require a photograph of a small child with the product. Avoid taking a picture that looks posed -- the more realistic and spontaneous your picture looks, the better. It is best if the people in the picture look happy. Sponsors don't like to see people angry or unhappy with their product.

For some contests you will be required to write a caption for the photograph. The best way to keep the judge's attention is to keep the caption brief. A good general rule is "shorter is better." It should be concise and clear.

It is a good idea to write your name and address on the back of the photograph. Sometimes this is even required in the rules. Then if your photograph is misplaced, the judges will still know who it is from. The judges cannot select your photograph as a winner if a name cannot be connected with it.

When mailing your entry, take care to see that it gets there in good condition. Place the picture between pieces of cardboard, and keep it secure with rubber bands or tape. Mail it in a sturdy envelope with the words "PHOTOGRAPH ENCLOSED-DO NOT BEND OR FOLD" printed on the outside. A folded, wrinkled, or torn photograph is unlikely to impress the judges.

PAY CONTESTS

Beware of pay contests. They are run like state lotteries -- their objective is to make money. They are legal, and are frequently run honestly. But when you enter, you are taking a risk. Often, there are multilevel tie-breakers, and to continue playing a contestant may be required to pay several more "entry fees." In general, we do not recommend these contests. If you want to enter one, read the rules carefully first.

Conclusion

As with sweepstakes, the most important thing to remember in entering contests is to always follow the rules. Even the best entry in a contest can never be a winner if you print it on a four-by-six-inch card when the rules call for a three-by-five-inch card, or if the entry is hand-written when the rules specify that it be printed. Before anything else, be certain that your entry conforms to the rules precisely.

Anyone can win contests. You do not have to have special skills or a college degree. Be creative and be willing to practice. It may take a few losing entries before you catch the knack. But if you put your mind to it, and are willing to put in the time, you can become a winner.

11. The Lotteries

The only thing you leave to chance is the lottery.
-Ernest Hemingway while visiting France

Since the revival of lotteries began in 1963 in New Hampshire, lotteries have spread into more than twenty states and the District of Columbia. In 1984, lotteries generated over $7 billion of revenues. To put that into perspective, that works out to over thirty dollars annually for every man, woman, and child in the United States.

Lotteries are currently enjoying their greatest acceptance and participation in history. However, lotteries have not always enjoyed such success.

A Brief History of Lotteries

There is very little that is new about lotteries. In fact, lotteries date back to ancient times. The word "lot," which refers to an object used in deciding a matter of chance, is believed to be of Teutonic origin, derived from "Hleut," meaning a pebble, bean, or token used to settle disputes or divide property.

Augustus Caesar sponsored the first known public lottery to raise funds to repair Rome. Guests at Roman banquets were often awarded door prizes via a lottery. Nero awarded prizes of slaves and country estates.

In 1539 Francis I of France established La Lotto di Firenze, the first regular cash-prize government lottery to raise funds for public works. Queen Elizabeth chartered an English lottery in

1566 to finance the Virginia Colony.

Lottery tickets were sold in England (1612-1621) to subsidize the Jamestown settlement. Later the colonies themselves used lottery revenues to finance the construction of churches, schools, buildings, bridges, roads, lighthouses, and port facilities.

On November 1, 1776, the Continental Congress implemented plans for the first national lottery sponsored by the United States of America. The plan was to use a lottery to raise over one million dollars to support the colonial Army. Although the lottery produced less than the projected revenues, it did provide the young country with working capital.

In the century following ratification of the Constitution, lotteries skyrocketed in popularity. Ticket vendors became more numerous that blacksmiths. Ticket agents were more common than taverns. It has been estimated that New York and Philadelphia each had over 150 lottery offices in 1833. Several universities, including Columbia, Yale, and Princeton, used lotteries to subsidize or finance construction.

As lotteries increased in popularity so did the number and magnitude of lottery scandals. Sponsors and promoters were found to be acting in bad faith. Some were blatant cheaters. Corrupt promoters controlled the drawings and saw to it that the most valuable prizes were never awarded. Some promoters "skipped town" without ever holding drawings.

In 1883, with support from the Quakers, Pennsylvania was the first state to outlaw lotteries. In less than fifty years, lotteries went from the nation's primary recreational activity to near extinction.

Modern American Lotteries

State lotteries were integrated in American culture in much the same way that America itself started. Modern American lotteries originated in the Northeast. New Hampshire was the first state to run a lottery. New York the second. The first lotteries were implemented in a conservative fashion. Advertising and sales of tickets were closely guarded.

The original New Hampshire lottery was referred to as a sweepstakes. Of course, by definition, state lotteries are not sweepstakes because they require a consideration in order to participate. The word sweepstakes was used because of the popularity of the Irish Sweepstakes (which is in fact, a lottery). The original New Hampshire lottery had little in common with today's sophisticated lottery game formats.

There were only two drawings per year. Customers paid three dollars for a ticket. The winning tickets were chosen based on the outcome of races at the Rockingham Race Track. By law, the state lottery could not advertise. Not surprisingly, the lottery generated meager revenues and floundered until 1985 when an instant scratch game was a big success and surpassed $15 million in gross revenues. New Hampshire's lottery revenues doubled for each of the next three years.

Strapped for funds, the New York state legislature approved its lottery in 1967. At first, lottery tickets could be sold only at banks and hotels. The main selling theme was that the lottery would be used to augment revenues for the state's schools. It was quickly realized that "greed," not "generosity," sold lottery tickets and the advertising theme was changed accordingly.

In the early 1970's New Jersey became the first state to generate big time revenues when it implemented a version of the racket's illegal numbers game. The remainder of the New England states eventually signed onto the lottery bandwagon. And Massachusetts became the most sophisticated lottery marketing state in the country using a plethora of continually changing lottery game formats.

The tight grip that restricted how lottery tickets were sold and advertised was loosened as the lotteries proved to be profitable and trustworthy. In 1974, Congress amended the regulations that curtailed lottery advertising nationwide.

In the mid-1970's New York hit the jackpot with the 6/36 lotto game in which lottery players bet 6 numbers out of 36 at astronomical odds (see odds chart). The lure of the million dollar super-prize led to new lottery revenue records.

The state lotteries today have learned well from the mistakes of the past. Nearly every precaution possible has been taken to guarantee that the lotteries are run honestly. Credibility, they know, is one of their prime commodities. The marketing departments of every state lottery know that a major scandal could cost them tens of millions of dollars or put them out of business entirely.

Lotteries have become an accepted part of life in America. Today, lottery winners are regularly featured on television news programs, and large jackpots are a frequent topic of conversation at work places and parties. In fact, lotteries have become so pervasive that in October of 1983, ABC television aired a series entitled *Lottery*. The show failed but the concept was so popular with the American public, that the premiere episode finished in the top 20 rated programs that week.

How Lotteries Operate

The operation of most state lotteries is fairly straightforward. Each lottery must have a method for recording entries. Until the computer explosion, most lottery tickets had two parts. One part would be entered in a drawing; the other was retained as a receipt. The lottery tickets then were collected, pooled, and mixed in a container from which the winning numbers would be drawn. In most lotteries, it was the bettor's responsibility to check whether he or she had won.

In a majority of the newer lottery games, computers are used to record entries to ensure that each entry has an equal chance of winning. Despite the use of computers, most states still require winners to identify themselves.

In the 1980's lottery marketing reached a new level in sophistication. Prize structures were tested for maximum player participation. Advertising campaigns rivalled that of any top brand product. In nearly every state with a lottery, the lottery has achieved widespread popular support. According to *The First Really Important Survey of American Habits* by Mel Poretz and Barry Sinrod (Price Stearn Sloan 1989), 79% of all Americans have bought a lottery ticket.

Lottery Winners

There seems to be a story to go with every million-dollar winner. In 1981, for example, Louis Eisenberg, after winning $5 million in the New York Lottery, quit his job as light bulb changer and began living the good life. The win made Lou a national celebrity and a guest on the Tonight Show with Johnny Carson. When New York police detective Robert Cunningham won the New York lottery he kept a promise to split the $6 million jackpot with a waitress from a local pizza parlor, who had helped pick out the numbers. In September 1984, Michael Witkowski won the largest lottery jackpot to date in the Illinois Lotto Game. The Illinois airports experienced one of their heaviest traffic days ever as thousands flew in to take a shot at the $40 million megaprize. About 80 million tickets in all were purchased. When Nancy and Glenn Squire of New Jersey forgot to bring their lotto numbers to the local lottery agent, they decided to let the computer select numbers for them. One of the eight tickets they purchased returned $2.2 million. The Squires learned that it sometimes pays to forget.

Most lottery winners insist that the money won't change their lives. However, few lives remain the same after large wins. When Curtis Sharp, Jr., won $5 million in the New York lottery, within one year he remarried and purchased a new $175,000 house and a new Cadillac. Many lottery winners retire early. Some bachelor and bachelorette winners have received scores of marriage proposals.

Winning a lottery is, however, not as easy as the state lottery commissions would like you to believe. In fact, the purpose of the lotteries is not to make you rich, as some advertising seems to imply. The state's reasons for running lotteries is to generate income for the state.

Lottery jackpot winners are not the only lottery winners. The annual report for the Illinois Lottery reported that $495 million worth of lottery tickets had been purchased in 1983 from the state. Of that amount, $231 million or 46.8 percent of the total lottery revenues was awarded in prizes. After operating expenses, the lottery made a profit of $215 million (43.8 percent of the total lottery revenues). Illinois uses lottery profits for its General Revenue Fund, which among other uses, benefits education and human services. Most of the other states with lotteries also apply lottery profits to the general funds. Several states direct the lottery funds specifically to education. In April 1985, to explain the use of lottery revenues, the New Jersey lottery ran a campaign entitled "Where the Money Goes." Of New Jersey lottery revenues, 50 percent is used for prizes, 10 percent covers overhead expenses and 40 percent is used for public programs.

Lottery Criticisms

- Lotteries are an inefficient manner to generate tax revenues. Of the net revenue after prize winnings, about 30% is spent on administration (media advertising, marketing consultants and computer and support services, commissions to sales agents).

- No form of gambling - legal or illegal - returns less to bettors. Of every dollar wagered on a lottery, approximately 50 cents is re-distributed to players as winnings. In contrast, most Las Vegas games return more than 90% of the gross monies wagered to players as winnings. Jai alai returns 80%. Horse racing returns 80%. Dog racing returns 80%.

- Lotteries are marketed as the "way out" of inner city problems, a kind of anti-work ethic. For lottery players, lotteries create more economic problems than they solve.

- The Chances of Winning Are Overstated (or unstated). Unlike commercially sponsored sweepstakes and contests, federal regulation of lottery promotions is weak. Since lotteries are both sponsored and run by the state governments, the situation is analogous to the wolf guarding the sheep.

- The Value of Prizes Is Overstated. In American lotteries winning $1 million is not winning $1 million cash. The million-dollar prizes are generally spread out at $50,000 per year for twenty years ($50,000 times 20 equals $1 million). In Canadian lotteries, prizes are handed out in one lump sum and they are tax-free. In fact, a $1 million prize does not cost a state lottery $1 million.

  Each year the spending power of a prize of $50,000 per year for 20 years will erode. At 6% annual inflation, after 10 years, $50,000 will be worth $28,000 in today's dollars. After 20 years, $50,000 will be worth only $15,600 in today's dollars.

For little more than $400,000, the states can purchase annuities that will pay the funds. Alan Richman of the Boston Globe summed up the matter succinctly when he wrote: "There is a lot of difference between...a million now and...a million over a period of twenty years. Both make you happy, but one makes you filthy rich." For the most part, large lottery prizes are annuities purchased by the state.

In major league sports, an athlete is considered a millionaire only when he receives a million dollars for a single season. In the real world, a person is considered a millionaire when he has a net worth greater than one million dollars. State lotteries winners are termed "millionaires" if they receive the winnings spread out over 20 years! Would you consider yourself a millionaire if you won a prize of one dollar per year for one million years? Probably not. And state lottery millionaires usually are not.

12. Lottery Strategies

I believe the overwhelming majority of people are sophisticated enough to recognize just how remote their chances of winning are and will act sensibly.
- Joseph Addabbo, late New York congressman who introduced a bill proposing a national lottery to fund social security.

People play for fun not to get rich.
My job is to run the best lottery I know how and not to be a moralist.
- James Hosker, Executive Director of the Massachusetts State Lottery.

Perhaps Representative Addabbo was right when he said that most people will exercise self-control, but many people do not understand lottery odds and just how remote the chances of winning are. Unfortunately, not every piece of printed lottery material expressly states the odds. And when the odds are stated, the information is printed in such small type that few people give it the attention it deserves. And the most important piece of information, the average prize value of each lottery ticket, is not readily given and can only be determined by a series of computations.

Fortunately, as in game sweepstakes, it is relatively easy to analyze lotteries. But before we show you how to perform the analyses, we would like to discuss how the most popular lottery formats -- instant-win lottery tickets and lotto games -- work.

Instant-Win Lottery Tickets

Instant-win lottery tickets work very much like instant-win game sweepstakes. Both have fixed odds and both let you know immediately whether you have won or lost. The only significant differences are:

- Lottery tickets generally cost $1. Sweepstakes game pieces cost only the price of two postage stamps.
- The average prize value of a $1 lottery ticket is forty to sixty cents. The average prize value of a sweepstakes game piece can vary between a fraction of a penny and $25.
- Sweepstakes are sponsored by private companies for promotional reasons. Lotteries are sponsored by state governments to make money (see Massachusetts lottery advertisment on next page).

Lotto

The lottery game that has most captivated the public's imagination is "lotto." In one lotto format, entrants select six numbers between one and forty (Canadians call this 6/40). The number of numbers that the entrant must "choose" and "choose from" varies from state to state.

Lotto's major appeal to players is based on its virtually unlimited prizes. Unlike most other lottery games, lotto is a pari-mutuel game (if there is more than one winner, the winners split the prize), and the prizes available to players depend upon weekly sales and the number of winners in each prize category. One additional characteristic is the rollover feature; if a drawing produces no grand prize winner, most of the jackpot is carried over and added to the next grand prize pool. The amount of cash offered in the lotto grand prize pool continues to increase until there is a grand prize winner.

Numbers Game

The numbers game is similar to lotto in that it too has pari-mutuel payoffs. The numbers game, however, offers considerably lower jackpots but better chances of winning. In the numbers game, players pick a three- or four-digit number. If the player is able to guess the winning number, he or she wins a share of the prize pool. In the four-digit game, since there are only 10,000 different combinations (0000 through 9999), there are usually winners in each game.

Understanding Lottery Odds

Many players believe that $1 lottery tickets are great buys. Where else, players reason, can you get a chance to win so much for so little? Indeed, if you are receiving some entertainment value from lottery tickets, perhaps they are a good buy. On the other hand, if you are playing lotteries strictly to win money, then you should be aware of the differences between price and value. If you spend five dollars for a widget that is worth only one dollar, you are getting less value than you would be paying ten dollars for a high-quality widget worth ten dollars. State-sponsored lottery tickets are sold at low prices but are generally a poor value. You can determine the value of a lottery ticket by dividing the summed total value of all the prizes by the number of lottery tickets printed. This calculation is analogous to the the calculations shown in Chapter 5 for game sweepstakes.

As an example, the $1 price of Connecticut's "Win For Life" instant-win lottery ticket is greater than its fifty-six-cent value. Purchasing this ticket is like getting two quarters, a nickel, and a penny in exchange for each $1 ticket you buy.

Table 12.1 shows the odds provided for the Connecticut "Win For Life" Instant-Win Lottery Game

The price of a lottery ticket is known. Unknown, but easily calculated, is the value of a lottery ticket. The average prize value of a lottery ticket is the total prize value divided by the number of lottery tickets printed. These calculations are similar to those for the sweepstakes game cards.

- Number of lottery tickets printed. For any given prize, multiply the number of prizes offered times the odds of winning that prize. This value should be the same for each prize.

Table 12.1

# OF PRIZES		ODDS OF WINNING		# OF LOTTERY TICKETS PRINTED
2,340,000	x	1: 7.7	=	18,000,000
252,000	x	1: 71.4	=	18,000,000
99,000	x	1: 182	=	18,000,000
11,520	x	1: 1,563	=	18,000,000
140	x	1: 128,571	=	18,000,000
40	x	1: 450,000	=	18,000,000
9	x	1: 2,000,000	=	18,000,000
1	x	1:18,000,000	=	18,000,000
1	x	1:18,000,000	=	18,000,000
1	x	1:18,000,000	=	18,000,000
1	x	1:18,000,000	=	18,000,000
16	x	1: 1,125,000	=	18,000,000

# of instant-win lottery tickets printed = 18,000,000

- The total prize value is the combined dollar value of all the prizes. For each different prize, multiply the number of each prize offered by the value of the prize. Add these numbers together.

Table 12.2, WIN FOR LIFE

PRIZES		# OF PRIZES		
$2	x	2,340,000	=	$4,680,000
$5	x	252,000	=	$1,260,000
$10	x	99,000	=	$ 990,000
$50	x	11,520	=	$ 576,000
$1000	x	140	=	$ 140,000
$10,000	x	40	=	$ 400,000
$1,000/week for life*	x	9	=	$1,800,000
$1,000/week for life*	x	1	=	$ 200,000
$20,000	x	1	=	$ 20,000
$15,000	x	1	=	$ 15,000
$10,000	x	1	=	$ 10,000
$5,000	x	16	=	$ 80,000
total prize value =				$10,171,000

The minimum prize awarded for the $1,000/week for life is $200,000.

The Average value of one instant-win lottery ticket is the total prize value divided by the number of lottery tickets printed. In this case, the value of one instant-win ticket is $0.56 ($10,171,000/18,000,000).

Since the $1 price of the WIN FOR LIFE instant-win lottery ticket is greater than its 56 cents value, the instant-win is not a good buy. Purchasing this instant win ticket is like getting 2 quarters, a nickel and a penny in exchange for your dollar.

Lotteries are run much like casino operations. The state must take in more money than it gives out in prizes so that it can make a profit. For this reason, you would not expect to find an instant-win lottery ticket with a prize value greater than its price.

Pari-Mutuel Lottery Odds

In the pari-mutuel lottery games like lotto and the numbers game, the state takes its money "off the top." Each state collects all the money from the tickets purchased, deducts its 50 percent, and then splits the prize money (and any remaining prize money from the previous drawing) among the winners. Since each state takes its money first, the state can never lose money in a lotto game.

The odds against winning a share of the top prize in lotto games are fantastic. Again, you have to choose six correct numbers (in any order). The greater the range of numbers you have to pick from, the more difficult it is to win. In other words, picking six numbers from one through forty is less of a long shot than picking six numbers from one through forty-four. Table 12.3 shows the lotto odds for several of the state lottery games. Notice that the Delaware game is approximately twelve times easier to win than the Illinois and New York games.

Table 12.3

TYPE OF LOTTO GAME	ODDS OF WINNING A SHARE OF JACKPOT	STATES
Picking 5 out of 40	658,007:1	DC, RI
Picking 6 out of 30	593,774:1	DE
Picking 6 out of 36	1,947,791:1	CT, MA
Picking 6 out of 39	3,262,622:1	NJ
Picking 6 out of 40	3,838,379:1	MD, MI, OH, PA, WA
Picking 6 out of 44	7,059,051:1	IL, NY
Picking 6 out of 48	12,273,532:1	NY

The pari-mutuel games are for players who love to take chances. In these games, you are not only taking a chance on winning, but also on how much you might win.

Not all jackpots are large. On December 16, 1984, eleven New York lotto players had to split a $20 million jackpot. Since the prizes are spread out over twenty years, each winner will receive $90,000 yearly. On September 29, 1984, twenty-one other ticket holders split a $4 million jackpot -- $190,540 over twenty years, or a mere $9,527 per year for the next twenty years. In April of 1985, the Massachusetts Megabucks Game (6/36 lotto) offered "super mini-bucks" prizes. Eighteen winners split a jackpot of $625,338. Since the jackpot was so small, the state awarded the entire prize at one time rather than spreading it out over twenty years. The one-time payment was $35,000. If the payments had been spread out over twenty years, as the above prizes were, the winners would have received only $1,750 each year! Such small payments are a very poor payoff given the long odds against winning.

In November of 1988, sixty persons picked the winning Massachusetts MegaBucks numbers (1-4-5-6-8-9). The expected jackpot shrunk from $5 million to just $6,100. One of the lottery winners said, "It went from a wonderful feeling - winning $5 million - to a letdown. I'm still happy, but disappointed - justifiably, I'd say."

Most lotto prizes are not that small. The Illinois lotto once awarded a $40 million prize to a single winner. New York also once awarded $20 million to a single winner. But of course the toughest part of the lottery is overcoming the tremendous odds to pick a winning number. If you are going to win a lotto prize, it is much better to win a big one and not have to share it.

How to Increase Your Odds of Winning Big in Lotto

In 1981, Professor Herman Chernoff, a professor of mathematics at MIT, issued a report on the Massachusetts lottery entitled "An Analysis of the Massachusetts Numbers Game." The Massachusetts Numbers Game allows players to make several different kinds of picks, including three- and four-digit numbers in and out of order. The state takes 40 percent from the day's pot and distributes the remainder on a pari-mutuel basis. Since the number of winners affects the size of the winnings in pari-mutuel systems, it is better to be the sole winner. Assuming that each number has an equal chance of winning, in the long run a player can increase the value of a pick if he or she bets only on unpopular numbers (those that are bet least frequently).

Chernoff constructed a sophisticated model that produced a portfolio of these preferred unpopular numbers in Massachusetts lottery. His study revealed that players had certain biases. For example, numbers with a one in them were overplayed, while numbers with zeros, nines, and repeated digits were underplayed. Chernoff projected that betting on his preferred numbers would produce an expected 8.6 percent return.

Again, the key to winning the numbers game and lotto is to bet on unpopular numbers. To discover which numbers and patterns of numbers are unpopular in your state's lottery, you must analyze the numbers that have won, the number of tickets purchased, and the number of winners. Do not look for numbers that have won recently. Look for numbers or patterns of numbers that, when they have won, have paid larger-than-average payoffs. For example, you should not bet on numbers that are in the news, because many of your competitors will likely be betting those numbers (1-7-7-6 is a bad number to bet in a numbers game around Independence Day).

The number 8888 was wagered on heavily on August 8, 1988. According to a Massachusetts lottery spokesman, $59,353.50 of the $1.3 million bet on that day was on 8888. Had the number won, the payoff would have been a pittance. The Pennsylvania State lottery shut down playing of the number 4,192 on September 12, 1985 because it was overplayed when Pete Rose closed in becoming baseball's all-time hit leader.

Also, numbers published in tip sheets for lottery players should be avoided. If the number did win, the payoff would be low. Many players bet yesterday's number. Again, you should not.

It is not a good idea to bet on the same number twice in one pari-mutuel game. If you bet this way and win, you will either be splitting a jackpot with yourself or at best be getting an extra share of a jackpot you have helped to divide into smaller pieces.

Because many lottery players use birth dates and ages of children to select their lottery numbers, numbers less than 31 are more frequently bet. To increase the size of your potential jackpot, consider betting on some of the higher numbers.

Unlike the pari-mutuel numbers game, the New York Pick-3 and Pick-4 lottery games offer fixed pay-offs (500:1 for Pick-3 and 5000:1 for Pick-4). It does not matter how many other players select the winning combination, the pay-off is always the same. For this reason, there is no way to improve either your odds of winning or your potential pay-off by betting underplayed numbers.

Occasionally a player will discover a special strategy applicable to his or her state lottery that can be extremely effective. For instance, a Maine shopkeeper detected a pattern in the sequence of lottery tickets that enabled him to dramatically increase his chances of winning. This strategy resulted in 29,000 winners instead of the 5,400 projected by the Maine lottery. Unfortunately, the state lotteries are now careful not to print lottery tickets with detectable patterns.

Strategies That Do Not Improve Your Chances

There are psychics who claim they can predict winning lottery numbers for you. Maybe they can. However, we can't name a single psychic who has won a $1 million jackpot in any of the state lotteries. Of course if enough psychics made lottery predictions, one would eventually win. But unless the event were repeatable, it would prove nothing.

Numerology systems that produce personal lottery numbers not only do not work but they don't make sense. Since only one set of numbers can win, of what value is a set of "personal" lottery numbers. Only the set of "winning" lottery numbers gets paid.

Many lotto players have formulated their own "systems" for choosing numbers. Often winners base their numbers on birth dates, ages, and anniversaries. Do not be misguided. The ratio of winners to losers is the same for those who use these systems as for those who do not. The losers simply do not get media attention. Any thorough statistical analysis of the state lottery games reveals that there is no way to predict future winning numbers based on past results. In a four-digit numbers game (0000-9999), there is a one-in-ten-thousand chance that on any given day, the same number will be drawn as the day before. Such coincidences have occurred, but no more often than one would statistically expect. On May 17, 1985, the same number, 0705, was selected for the second consecutive day in the Massachusetts Numbers Game. Of course, because so many people tend to pick the same number that won the day before, twice as many people had bet on the number on the second day. Each winner received half as much money for the win as the previous day's winners.

The Only 100% Guaranteed Method to Win the Lottery Every Day

There is only one guaranteed method to win the lottery -- don't play. If you don't play, the monies that your state makes from other people playing will subsidize your tax bill. Depending on where you live you stand to win approximately $15 to $80 or more per year - guaranteed. Nearly everyone who objects publicly to lotteries does so on moral grounds. We're not. We're advising that you should not play because lotteries are poor bets -- period.

The television stations that air lottery drawings live want you to play so they get big viewer ratings. Your lottery commissioner and everyone associated with the lottery want you to play because their jobs depend on people playing. People who produce how to win lottery materials want you to play because they want you to buy their books and products. Lotteries are not mentioned in the title of this book (even though we have been told it would help to sell more copies) because the truth is ... lotteries are poor bets. You may not hear it from anyone else but you've been warned.

If You Must Play, Tips On Lotteries

If, despite our admonishments and the negative return on investment, you decide to play lotteries, be certain that you at least get some enjoyment value out of playing. Never play your lottery tickets alone. Make playing your lottery tickets a family event. Purchase the fewest number of tickets that you must. Enjoy the game. Enjoy knowing that you are subsidizing the state's tax liabilities. And use the tips below to minimize your expected losses. With some random chance acting in your favor, maybe you'll hit a jackpot. But remember that in the long run, it is a better bet not to play at all.

- Concentrate your lotto entries on drawings with jackpots near record levels. When carryover jackpots are high, the average prize value of each entry goes up.

- Not all lottery games have the same odds or the same negative return on investment. Look for the games with the less negative return on investment.

- Always play free lottery tickets. Several states mail coupons good for free tickets in order to lure you into playing.

- In order to avoid losing your tickets, always store them in the same place.

- If you win big, consult an accountant before signing your winning ticket. The accountant may be able to find ways to lessen your tax burden.

- Save losing lottery tickets and keep a record of all lottery ticket purchases. When you win, you can deduct the cost of your losing tickets from your winnings in computing taxes.

  Sometimes you can also enter losing tickets in special second-chance drawings run by the state lottery. In 1987, Massachusetts McDonald's accepted losing lottery tickets as 50 cent coupons on salads. In some states, the local television station that carries lottery drawings on live television sometimes run sweepstakes where losing lottery tickets are the required official entry form.

- Do not procrastinate about claiming your winnings. In most states, you have one year to claim your prize or it reverts to the state. If you check the annual report of your state's lottery commission, you will find that thousands of dollars go unclaimed. A procrastinating New Jersey winner showed up to collect his $100,000 prize one year and one day after the drawing and he lost his entire prize because he was one day late.

- Beware of foreign lotteries such as the Irish Sweepstakes. Many of the tickets to these lotteries sold in the United States are forgeries.

- Know how the lottery is played. Instruction booklets are available from most lottery sales agents. For more information, write to your state's lottery commission (see Appendix C).

- Always check winning numbers. If you should miss an announcement of winning numbers, visit your local lottery ticket agent, or write to your state's lottery commission. If your state doesn't have a lottery, there are several subscription lottery magazines and newsletters that provide lists of winning lottery numbers and addresses for more information.

If You Are Fortunate Enough To Win A Large Lottery Prize

- See an estates attorney. You are now a primary target for con artists and scams.
- Put aside one-third for taxes.
- Make a wish list. Splurge but don't go crazy. Buy only the things you really want.
- Avoid lending money. Lending money is a quick and easy way to lose your friends.
- Don't make any major financial decisions right away.
- Get an investment adviser.

13. Winning Sweepstakes in Action

Winners always sleep well. - Benjamin Cohen

Winning sweepstakes is a lot like fishing. Like fishing holes, no two sweepstakes are quite the same. Sometimes you will catch a big fish. Sometimes a small fish. Sometimes no fish at all. Of course, if you choose the wrong hole, or use the wrong bait and the wrong equipment, your chances of catching fish will be quite small. Likewise for sweepstakes.

Don't let anyone tell you that a prize competition is a prize competition is a prize competition. Sweepstakes, contests, and lotteries are very different. And furthermore, sweepstakes entries submitted to the better sweepstakes have a much better chance of winning than entries submitted to lesser sweepstakes. This has been proven time and again. If you pick your sweepstakes according to the criteria in this book, you will win better prizes and more often.

Finding the best sweepstakes is not enough. You must also be ready to enter at all times! Play it S-A-F-E! *S*elect Carefully. *A*ct Quickly. *F*ollow the rules. *E*nter often.

And finally, we want to hear from you! We love hearing about your sweepstakes successes! And, to keep abreast of the latest sweepstakes, we invite you to try our WINNING SWEEPSTAKES NEWSLETTER. A subscription card can be found in the back of this book.

If the card is missing, send a brief note mentioning this book and requesting a sample. Please enclose a #10 self-addressed, stamped envelope and mail to:

WINNING SWEEPSTAKES NEWSLETTER
Proven Strategy Sample Offer
P.O. Box 1468
Framingham, MA 01701

To sweepstakes players everywhere, we wish you success!

Your Sweepstakes Success Partners,

Jeff and Robin

Jeffrey and Robin Sklar

Appendix A: Derivation of the Winning Sweepstakes Formulas

On page 68 of the book we utilize one of our two Winning Sweepstakes formulas. The following formulas apply for all sweepstakes. However, only in game sweepstakes will you be able to determine the exact number of entries and therefore be able to perform precisely all the following calculations. In random draw sweepstakes, you must be able to estimate the number of entries in order to use the formulas.

L = Total number of losing entries in a given sweepstakes.

W = Total number of winning entries in a given sweepstakes.

P = Total number of entries submitted to a given sweepstakes. (In game sweepstakes, "P" is the number of game pieces printed.)

N = Your chance of winning a prize with one entry in a given sweepstakes.

C = Your chance of winning at least one prize based on submitting "S" entries to a given sweepstakes.

S = Number of entries you submit to a given sweepstakes.

1. Every entry is either a winner or loser.

$$L + W = P$$

Stated otherwise, the percentage of losers plus the percentage of winners equals 100% (or 1).

$$\frac{L}{P} + \frac{W}{P} = 1$$

2. Your chances of winning with one entry equals the number of winning entries (W) divided by the number of total entries (P).

$$N = \frac{W}{P}$$

3. The chance that every entry you submit ("S") will lose is:

$$\left(\frac{L}{P}\right)^{S}$$

4. Your chance of winning at least one prize plus your chance of not winning any prizes equals 100% (or 1).

$$C + \left(\frac{L}{P}\right)^{S} = 1$$

Through algebraic manipulation, your chances of winning at least one prize is stated in this way:

$$C = 1 - \left(\frac{L}{P}\right)^{S}$$

This is **FORMULA #1**.

FORMULA #1 can be used to determine your chances of winning a given sweepstakes based on the specific number of entries you intend to submit.

To state the above equation in another way:

$$1 - C = \left(\frac{L}{P}\right)^{S}$$

Logarithms are used to solve the "S" exponential.

$$\text{Log } (1 - C) = S \times \text{Log}\left(\frac{L}{P}\right)$$

or

$$S = \frac{\text{Log } (1 - C)}{\text{Log}\left(\frac{L}{P}\right)}$$

Given that $\frac{L}{P} = 1 - \frac{W}{P}$ and that $\frac{W}{P} = N$

then ... $\frac{L}{P} = 1 - N$

Because of this, the formula

$$S = \frac{\text{Log }(1 - C)}{\text{Log}\left(\frac{L}{P}\right)}$$

can also be stated in this way:

$$S = \frac{\text{Log }(1 - C)}{\text{Log }(1 - N)}$$

This is **FORMULA #2**.

Formula #2 can be used to determine the number of entries you need to submit to have a specific chance of winning a given sweepstakes.*

To arrive at the general formula to determine the number of entries needed to have a 50 percent chance of winning a given sweepstakes, let C = .5. In that case, the formula will appear in this way:

$$S = \frac{\text{Log }(1 - .5)}{\text{Log }(1 - N)} = \frac{-.30103}{\text{Log }(1 - N)}$$

* Note: Most hand-held calculators have a built in logarithm function which you can use to easily compute the values of "S".

Addresses for the State Attorney Generals

ALABAMA Attorney General
11 S. Union Street
Montgomery, AL 36130

ALASKA Attorney General
Dept. of Law
P.O. Box K
Juneau, AK 99811

ARIZONA Attorney General
1275 W. Washington
Phoenix, AZ 85007

ARKANSAS Attorney General
201 E. Markham St., Suite 510
Little Rock, AR 72201

CALIFORNIA Attorney General
Dept. of Justice
1515 K St., Suite 511
Sacramento, CA 95814

COLORADO Attorney General
Dept. of Law
1525 Sherman St., 3rd Fl.
Denver, CO 80203

CONNECTICUT Attorney General
Capitol Annex
30 Trinity Street
Hartford, CT 06106

DELAWARE Attorney General
Carvel State Off. Bldg.
820 N. French Street
Wilmington, DE 19801

DISTRICT OF COLUMBIA
Office of Corporation Counsel
1350 Pennsylvania Ave., NW
Room 329
Washington, DC 20004

FLORIDA Attorney General
Dept, of Legal Affairs
The Capitol
Tallahassee, FL 32301

GEORGIA Attorney General
State Law Dept.
132 State Judicial Bldg.
Atlanta, GA 30334

HAWAII Attorney General
State Capitol
Honolulu, HI 96813

IDAHO Attorney General
Off. of Attorney General
Statehouse
Boise, ID 83720

ILLINOIS Attorney General
500 S. Second Street
Springfield, IL 62706

INDIANA Attorney General
219 State House
Indianapolis, IN 46204

IOWA Attorney General
Hoover State Off. Bldg.
Des Moines, IA 50319

KANSAS Attorney General
Judicial Center
Topeka, KS 66612

KENTUCKY Attorney General
Atate Capitol
Frankfort, KY 40601

LOUISIANA Attorney General
Dept. of Justice
P.O. Box 94005
Baton Rouge, LA 70804

MAINE Attorney General
Dept. of the Attorney General
State House Station #6
Augusta, ME 04333

MARYLAND Attorney General
7 N. Calvert Street
Baltimore, MD 21202

MASSACHUSETTS Attorney General
One Ashburton Place
Boston, MA 02108

MICHIGAN Attorney General
525 W. Ottawa, Law Bldg.
Lansing, MI 48913

MINNESOTA Attorney General
102 State Capitol
St. Paul, MN 55155

MISSISSIPPI Attorney General
5th Fl., Gartin Bldg.
Jackson, MS 39201

MISSOURI Attorney General
Supreme Ct. Bldg.
P.O. Box 899
Jefferson City, MO 65102

MONTANA Attorney General
Dept. of Justice
215 N. Sanders St.
Helena, MT 59620

NEBRASKA Attorney General
Rm. 2115, State Capitol
P.O. Box 94906
Lincoln, NE 68509

NEVADA Attorney General
Heroes Memorial Bldg.
Capitol Complex
Carson City, NV 89710

NEW HAMPSHIRE Attorney General
208 State House Annex
235 Capitol Street
Concord, NH 03301

NEW JERSEY Attorney General
Dept. of Law & Public Safety
Justice Hughes Complex, CN080
Trenton, NJ 08625

NEW MEXICO Attorney General
Bataan Memorial Bldg.
P.O. Box 1508
Santa Fe, NM 87501

NEW YORK Attorney General
Dept. of Law
State Capitol
Albany, NY 12224

N. CAROLINA Attorney General
Dept. of Justice
Justice Bldg., Box 629
Raleigh, NC 27602

N. DAKOTA Attorney General
1st Fl., State Capitol
Bismarck, ND 58505

OHIO Attorney General
30 E. Broad St., 17th Fl.
Columbus, OH 43266

OKLAHOMA Attorney General
112 State Capitol
Oklahoma City, OK 73105

OREGON Attorney General
Dept. of Justice
100 State Off. Bldg.
Salem, OR 97310

PENNSYLVANIA Attorney General
Strawberry Sq., 16th Fl.
Harrisburg, PA 17120

RHODE ISLAND Attorney General
72 Pine Street
Providence, RI 02903

S. CAROLINA Attorney General
Dennis Bldg.
P.O. Box 11549
Columbia, SC 29211

S. DAKOTA Attorney General
3rd Fl., State Capitol
Pierre, SD 57501

TENNESSEE Attorney General
450 James Robertson Pkwy.
Nashville, TN 37219

TEXAS Attorney General
Box 12548, Capitol Station
Austin, TX 78711

UTAH Attorney General
236 State Capitol
Salt Lake City, UT 84114

VERMONT Attorney General
Pavilion Off. Bldg.
109 State Street
Montpelier, VT 05602

VIRGINIA Attorney General
Off. of the Attorney General
101 N. Eight Street, 5th Fl.
Richmond, VA 23219

WASHINGTON Attorney General
Temple of Justice
Olympia, WA 98504

WEST VIRGINIA Attorney General
Rm. E-26, State Capitol
Charleston, WV 25305

WISCONSIN Attorney General
Dept. of Justice
114 E. State Capitol
P.O. Box 7857
Madison, WI 53707

WYOMING Attorney General
State Capitol
Cheyenne, WY 82002

Addresses for the State Lottery Commissions

Arizona Lottery Commission
301 E. Virginia #1200
Phoenix, AZ 85004

California Lottery Commission
1303 J Street
Sacramento, CA 95814

Colorado Lottery Division
Dept. of Revenue
201 W. Eighth St., Rm. 600
Pueblo, CO 81003

Connecticut Division of Special Revenue
Dept. of Revenue Serices
Russell Road
Newington, CT 06111

Delaware State Lottery
Dept. of Finance
Suite 202, Blue Hen Mall
Dover, DE 19901

District Of Columbia
Lottery & Charitable Games Control Bd.
2401 Martin Luther King, SE
Washington, DC 20020

Florida State Lottery
Rm. 335, Carlton Bldg.
Tallahassee, FL 32399

Idaho Lottery Division
Revenue & Taxation Dept.
Statehouse
Boise, ID 83720

Illinois Dept. of the Lottery
201 E. Madison
Springfield, IL 62702

Iowa Lottery Commission
Dept. of Revenue & Finance
2015 Grand Avenue
Des Moines, IA 50312

Kansas State Lottery
1st Fl., State House
Topeka, KS 66612

Maine State Lottery Commission
Dept. of Finance
State House Station #30
Augusta, ME 04333

Maryland Lottery Agency
6776 Reisterstown Road
Baltimore, MD 21215

Massachusetts Lottery Commission
15 Rockdale Street
Braintree, MA 02184

Michigan Bureau of State Lottery
6545 Mercantile Way
P.O. Box 30023
Lansing, MI 48909

Minnesota Charitable Gambling Control Bd.
Rm. N475, Griggs Midway Bldg.
1821 University Avenue
St. Paul, MN 55104

Missouri State Lottery Commission
Dept. of Revenue
Trumam Bldg., Box 1603
Jefferson City, MO 65101

Montana Lottery
Dept. of Commerce
Capitol Station
Helena, MT 59620

Nebraska Charitable Gaming
Division
Dept. of Revenue
P.O. Box 94818
Lincoln, NE 68509

New Hampshire Sweepstakes
Commission
Ft. Eddy Street
Concord, NH 03301

New Jersey State Lottery
Commission
Treasury Dept., CN041
Trenton, NJ 08625

New York Division of Lottery
Empire State Plaza
Swan St. Bldg.
Albany, NY 12223

Ohio Lottery Commission
615 W. Superior Avenue
Cleveland, OH 44113

Oregon Oregon Lottery
2767 22nd St., SE
Salem, OR 97310

Pennsylvania Bur. of Lotteries
Dept. of Revenue
2850 Turnpike Industrial Rd.
Middletown, PA 17055

Rhode Island State Lottery
1425 Pontiac Avenue
Cranston, RI 02920

South Dakota Lottery
State Capitol
Pierre, SD 57501

Vermont Lottery Commission
58 E. State Srteet
Montpelier, VT 05602

Washington State Lottery
Commission
600 Park Village Plaza
1200 Cooper Pt. Rd.
Olympia, WA 98504

West Virginia State Lottery
Commission
State Capitol Complex
Charleston, WV 25305

Virginia Lottery Commission
2201 West Broad Street
Richmond, VA 23220

Microsoft Corporation
16011 NE 36th Way
Box 97017
Redmond, WA 98073-9717

Tel 206 882 8080
Telex 160520
Fax 206 883 8101

Microsoft
'I Want It All'
Sweepstakes

POWER
TIME
MONEY

September 22, 1989

Sebell, Robin

C O N G R A T U L A T I O N S!

As the independent judging organization administering the Microsoft "I Want It All" Sweepstakes, it is our pleasure to confirm that you have won a $1000 Shopping Spree at the store where you submitted your sweepstakes entry.

Please present this letter at

0660368
Computer Factory
50-60 Wooster Rd.
Framingham, MA 02173

by October 22, 1989. It entitles you to your choice of Microsoft products up to a value of $1000 at suggested retail price. We have enclosed a list of Microsoft products and suggested retail prices to aid you in your selections.

Your prize is redeemable one time only and is not transferable. Selections shall not exceed $1000 suggested retail price. No cash or credit will be given.

Because of the value of this prize, we are obliged to file IRS Form 1099 at the end of the year in which your prize is claimed. We will provide you with a copy of this form--all further tax reporting responsibilities are yours.

Again, on behalf of Microsoft Corporation, we offer you our most enthusiastic congratulations and our thanks for participating in the "I Want It All" Sweepstakes.

Cordially,

Peg Heetmann

Peg Heetmann
Promotion Marketing Services, Inc.

AFFIDAVIT OF ELIGIBILITY & RELEASE

State of__________________________________

County of__________________________________

I, ____________________________ being duly sworn, hereby state as follows: I am ________ years of age; I am a U.S. resident; my social security number is _____________________________; my telephone numbers are: at work or during the day ______________________________, at home_________________________. I am employed at____________________________________.

I am submitting this Affidavit with the understanding that it will be relied upon to determine my eligibility in the "I Want It All" Sweepstakes, sponsored by Microsoft Corporation. I have not been awarded any prize in the "I Want It All" Sweepstakes and I understand that, subject to determination of my eligibility to be a prize winner, I may not be a winner and that decisions of the promotion agency, Promotion Marketing Services, Inc., are final on all matters relating to this sweepstakes.

I understand that if I should become a qualified winner, I will be notified within 60 days.

I agree that if I should become a qualified winner, Microsoft Corporation will have, without further obligation to me, the right to use my sweepstakes entry, my name and my photograph or may use any taped appearance or interview with me in connection with the publicity, advertising and promotional activities of the "I Want It All" Sweepstakes.

I affirm and represent that I have complied with all the rules and regulations of this sweepstakes and that I have committed no fraud or deception in entering the sweepstakes or in claiming any prize. I further represent that I am not an employee of the sponsor, Microsoft Corporation, its affiliates, agencies, participating retailers, participating distributors or of any other entity stated in the official rules whose employees are not eligible to enter the sweepstakes or a member of the family of any such employee.

I understand and acknowledge and hereby, for myself, my heirs, executors and administrators, do waive and release any and all rights, claims and causes of action whatsoever I may have against the promotion agency and/or the sponsor of any matter, cause or things whatsoever arising out of my acceptance and utilization of the prize that I may win or have won in the "I Want It All" Sweepstakes. I also acknowledge that I am solely responsible for all federal, state and local taxes due as a winner of this game as well as obtaining and paying for any life, travel, accident, property or other insurance related to the use of the prize.

I agree to return upon demand to the sponsor any prize or the value of said prize which may be awarded to me if any statement made by me in this affidavit is false.

Sworn to me this________________day of_____________, 1989.

Notary Public

____

____
Signature

____
Address

____
City

____
State, Zip

2807 Lincoln Way
P.O. Box 898, Lynnwood
Washington, 98046

August 16, 1990

ROBIN SKLAR

Dear ROBIN SKLAR:

Congratulations! You have been selected in the Osco/Sav•On Second Chance Sweepstakes. You may be the winner of a **1/2 Cut Diamond Earrings.**

In order to verify you as a winner, it is required that you fill out, sign and return the attached Submission Agreement Form. Keep a copy for your files, and return the original form via certified mail.

The Submission Agreement Form must be received at my office absolutely no later than **August 29, 1990**. Failure to return the material by this date will result in disqualification.

If you have any questions, please don't hesitate to call me at (206) 742-0990.

Sincerely,

Joy Welever
Administrative Assistant

Enclosure

JLW

SUBMISSION AGREEMENT FORM

PROMOTION NAME: RED HOT COUPON BONANZA

PROMOTION SPONSOR: AMERICAN DRUG STORES

PRIZE BEING CLAIMED: 1/2 cut Diamond Fashion Earrings Retail Value: $ 575

Check Appropriate Item:

[ ] I am the individual claiming the prize.

[ ] The winner of the prize is under 18 years of age. As the individual claiming the prize I certify I am the parent or legal guardian of the prize winner.

PERSONAL DATA (Please print)

◊ Name: ______________________ Social Security #: ______________

◊ Address: ______________________________________

◊ Phone Number: Home: (____) ______________ Work: (____) ______________

◊ Current or Last Employer: ______________________________

◊ Employer's City & State: ______________________ Phone Number: (____) ______________

INFORMATION ON MY SPOUSE or PARENT (Circle one) IS AS FOLLOWS:

◊ Name: ______________________________________

◊ Address: ______________________________________

◊ Current or Last Place of Employment: ______________________________

◊ City and State of Employment: ______________________________

TAX RESPONSIBILITY

I understand that I am responsible for all Income tax liability on the prize won irregardless of the value. If the retail value of the price is $600 or above the sponsor of the promotion will file an information form with the I.R.S. identifying me as a recipient of the prize at the retail value shown above.

PUBLICITY RELEASE

If I am verified as a legitimate winner the promotion sponsor has my permission to publicize this fact and to use my name and/or picture in any of their advertising or promotion materials without further compensation.

LIABILITY RELEASE

I release AMERICAN DRUG STORES (sponsor) and TPI Promotional Marketing from any injury, death, damage, liability or loss I may suffer as a result of using or accepting the prize, or as a result of a malfunction of the prize.

AGREEMENTS & UNDERSTANDING

◊ I understand that I am not a winner until any game materials (if applicable) submitted and attached have been verified as valid winning materials and until it has been verified that I meet the conditions of eligibility in the Official Rules.

◊ I submit that the information on this form is true and accurate and that I am not an employee of the sponsor or any of the companies engaged in the development of the promotion.

◊ I understand that all materials submitted become the property of the sponsor and cannot be returned.

◊ I understand that according to the promotion rules, if the claims for prizes in any category exceed the number of prizes published for that category, then a drawing will be conducted from all those claiming prizes to award the correct published number of prizes for that category.

◊ I understand that failure to complete any portion of this form or failure to return per the instructions below may result in disqualification for the prize.

◊ I understand that if I am a Canadian citizen I must correctly answer a skill question as a condition of eligibility: The capital of Quebec is ______________________________

INSTRUCTIONS

1) Complete this form and sign below.
2) Retain a photocopy of this form and any attachment for your files.
3) Send the original of this form via certified mail to: TPI PROMOTIONAL MARKETING, P.O. BOX 898, LYNNWOOD, WA 98046.
4) This form must be returned to TPI no later than **AUGUST 31, 1990**.

SIGNATURE

Signature: ______________________________ Date: ______________

SPECIAL OPPORTUNITY TO START

Winning Sweepstakes

☐ Yes, I want to start winning now! Please begin my 1 year (12 issues) subscription to **WINNING SWEEPSTAKES NEWSLETTER** - listing your latest selection of choice sweepstakes and contests - for just $18 (regularly $24). Also send my free copy of the four page "**Special Report: The Guide To Winning Sweepstakes**". *It is clearly understood that if Winning Sweepstakes Newsletter doesn't live up to my expectations I may tell you to cancel at anytime and you will refund my original subscription payment - in full.*

☐ Check/Money Order enclosed   Charge my: ☐ Visa   ☐ MasterCard

Account # ______________________ Exp Date: __________

Signature ______________________

Name ______________________

Address ______________________

City/State/Zip ______________________

☐ Please send me a sample issue of **WINNING SWEEPSTAKES NEWSLETTER.**

Mail your payment to: **WINNING SWEEPSTAKES NEWSLETTER**
P.O. Box 1468 • Framingham, MA 01701

QMN10

PLACE
STAMP
HERE

Winning Sweepstakes
NEWSLETTER

P.O. Box 1468
Framingham, MA 01701

PLACE
STAMP
HERE

P.O. Box 1468
Framingham, MA 01701